Blowing your cover

1. Buy this Guide and a Media Pack

2. Watch Leader's Training DVD

3. Plan the Course

4. Order Workbooks

5. Run Blowing Your Cover

Blowing your cover

Leader's Guide

Mike Sprenger
and Kevin Higham

MONARCH
BOOKS

Oxford, UK & Grand Rapids, Michigan, USA

First published in the UK in 2006 by Monarch Books
(a publishing imprint of Lion Hudson plc),
Mayfield House, 256 Banbury Road, Oxford OX2 7DH
Tel: +44 (0) 1865 302750   Fax: +44 (0) 1865 302757
Email: monarch@lionhudson.com
www.lionhudson.com

ISBN-13: 978-1-85424-775-9 (UK)
ISBN-10: 1-85424-775-1 (UK)
ISBN-13: 978-0-8254-6138-5 (USA)
ISBN-10: 0-8254-6138-3 (USA)

Distributed by:
UK: Marston Book Services Ltd, PO Box 269,
Abingdon, Oxon OX14 4YN;
USA: Kregel Publications, PO Box 2607,
Grand Rapids, Michigan 49501.

The text paper used in this book has been made from
wood independently certified as having come from sustainable forests.

British Library Cataloguing Data
A catalogue record for this book is available from the British Library.

Printed and bound in Malta by Gutenberg Press.

Contents

Foreword

Unconditional Love

As statistics on church membership decrease in the United Kingdom and throughout Europe, Christians face a crucial challenge. The challenge is firstly to motivate and equip the body of Christ to present the gospel to a needy world. And secondly, to ask the question, "Do the people we are trying to reach understand what we are trying to tell them?" Blowing Your Cover addresses both these crucial aspects as it equips the believer with practical, down-to-earth tools as well as asking the important question, "Are we connecting with the people we are so desperate to reach?"

In the last two years, I have had an encounter with God that has helped shape my perception of evangelism. John 3:16 expresses this very clearly. "For God so loved the world that he gave his one and only Son …" It was love that motivated God into action. So what is evangelism? It starts when we have love in our hearts for the people around us and this love motivates us to step out into all sorts of responses and actions. Here is something profound and relevant for the post-modern mindset of today. In our sceptical, cynical world how will people know that the message of Jesus Christ is true? Answer, when they meet real love. For when they see our love and experience it, there will be openness to our words.

Let me encourage you with a metaphor: "Be a pastor to those around you." Love people unconditionally and always seek their spiritual welfare. The challenge for each of us is to ask God the specific question, "Who am I called to love?"

In 1 Corinthians, the apostle Paul talks of many things. He talks of faith, hope and love, but the greatest of these is love. I am convinced that Blowing Your Cover will equip you practically to express this love to the world around you.

Laurence Singlehurst
April 2006

Introduction

Welcome to your Blowing Your Cover Leader's Guide. This guide is designed to provide you with the notes and training necessary to teach Blowing Your Cover to your church.

The Guide and enclosed DVD will help you to deliver the course both confidently and effectively by using the step-by-step practical advice contained within it. However, we recognise that each church is unique and consequently we want you to put your stories, your illustrations, your personality and your church's "flavour" onto the Leader's Guide and deliver the course in the way that is unique to you and your church.

As authors, it has been a great privilege to run the course in many different churches, resulting in many changed lives. Yet, just as Elijah passed on a mantle to Elisha, we believe that in a similar way we are passing the mantle of equipping people in lifestyle evangelism to you. In the New Testament, Ephesians 4:11–12 states that God calls some people to be teachers and some to be evangelists in order to equip "God's people for works of service". This includes you; God wants to use you! God has called you to equip the body of Christ to be Good News to those around them. To assist you in the process we have included a 30-minute Leader's Training DVD within this pack that, as you watch it, will train you and your team to run the course.

Our prayer for you, as you join thousands of other Christians across the country, is that you too will see lives changed and many people saved and added to your local church!

Every blessing!

Mike Sprenger
Kevin Higham

PART ONE
Deployment

The following notes are taken from the Leader's Training DVD included in the front of the Leader's Guide and are designed to give you a brief synopsis of its content.

Please ensure that you and your team have watched the DVD. It is designed to be an essential tool in sharing the vision and heart behind the course. It will also talk you through effective deployment of Blowing Your Cover.

Remember, evangelism can be fun, so enjoy the course and watch what God will do.

Catch the vision

- Four and a half million people in the UK can make a difference if they are trained and equipped to share their faith effectively
- Imagine the difference you and your church can make
- Eighty percent of people come to faith through friends and family
- Let's not have "hit and run" evangelism
- Let's move evangelism from being a bolt-on option to church life, to being the centre of church life
- Encourage people to take a step of faith
- Lifestyle evangelism comes from your innermost being

Course overview

- Session One – Communicating the Gospel
- Session Two – Your Sphere of Influence
- Session Three – Connecting with Your Culture

- Session Four – The Impact of Your Life
- Session Five – A Spirit-filled Lifestyle
- Session Six – Blowing Your Cover

Vision principles

- Faith
- Learning
- Opportunities
- Empowering

Questions to consider

- Who will do the taining and where?
- How many trainers are you going to use?
- Who will you train?
- When will the training start?
- What do you want the outcome to be?

Seven keys of effective deployment

1. Cast the vision within your church
    - Amongst leaders and church members alike
2. Think through your teaching method
    - Central teaching – small-group seated
3. Implement as a team
    - Use a small team of gifted trainers to deliver the course

4. Plan and prepare
    - Add your stories, illustrations, personality and flavour of church
5. Keep session in order and on time
    - Each session builds on the previous one
6. Receive feedback
    - Aim to improve your and your team's delivery
7. Attend a Blowing Your Cover conference where appropriate
    - There is nothing like hearing from the Blowing Your Cover team first hand when they are in your area

Materials overview

- Leader's Guide
    - All leaders will need to make their guide their own!
- Leader's Guide DVD
    - Remember to have all your team watch this
- Media Pack
    - Contains video clips and slides that work with the Leader's Guide
- Workbook
    - All participants will need one
- BYC Conferences
    - Please check our website www.blowingyourcover.com

Finally, remember also to purchase the appropriate Blowing Your Cover resources, including the Media Pack, prior to attempting to run the course.

PART TWO
Walkthrough

This part of the Leader's Guide contains the Blowing Your Cover six-session walkthrough, which explains:

- What needs to be done at any given point in the training
- How to use the associated slides effectively
- Major principles that need to be brought out from each session
- Additional relevant scriptures

Important

Let your style, gifting and personality come across as you train others. However, remember that a good trainer also draws on the experiences and input of others.

Ensure the key principles of the course come through.

The term "group" is frequently used throughout the walkthrough section. For ease of writing, this could also refer to multiple groups.

Walkthrough symbols

To help you know what to do and when to do it we have used a set of symbols. These are shown as follows:

READ OUT

The "Read Out" box

Anything in a grey shaded area requires the leader to read out the text that appears there – including slides and Bible verses.

Please don't feel you have to recite the contents word for word; often it will be appropriate to paraphrase.

A SLIDE

A picture of the slide(s) is positioned in the run of the text so that the leader knows exactly where it should come in respect to the written material in the workbook.

If a slide appears within a "Read Out" box then read out the content of the slide also.

INSTRUCTIONS

Anything appearing under this symbol contains notes, tips, appropriate explanations and things to do during the session.

SO WHAT?

This represents the BYC "so what" principle. Anything appearing with this symbol contains foundational principles that need to be communicated, additional Bible verses or relevant applications.

Blowing your cover

Session 1

Communicating the Gospel

Pre-Session Notes

- The approximate time required for this session is one and a half hours, depending on the amount of time spent in group interaction.
- This session sets the tone for the rest of the course, so welcome discussion, group interaction and questions.
- Make sure you are familiar with the accompanying Media Pack, by watching all the session 1 media clips.
- Allow adequate time at the end of the session for people to practise presenting the gospel graphically.
- You also need extra sheets of paper for this session.

Welcome

START MEDIA PACK DVD SESSION ONE – WELCOME

READ OUT

AIMS

1. To understand the importance of the gospel
2. To be able to communicate the gospel visually
3. To be able to discern when a person is ready to become a Christian
4. To be able to lead that person to Jesus
5. To be sure of that person's conversion

Let us start by reminding ourselves of the main points of the gospel message.

The gospel

READ OUT

Mark 8:34–36

Then he called the crowd to him along with his disciples and said: "If anyone would come after me, he must deny himself and take up his cross and follow me. For whoever wants to save his life will lose it, but whoever loses his life for me and for the **gospel** will save it. What good is it for a man to gain the whole world, yet forfeit his soul?" (emphasis added)

INSTRUCTIONS

- Encourage people that opportunities to share their faith will come their way.
- Ask one member of the group to stand up and briefly explain the main points of the gospel in three minutes. Mention that many people have given their lives for the gospel. For instance, people such as the first disciples and Hudson Taylor, founder of the China Inland Mission, who lost his wife and four of his children.

- Then ask, "So what is this gospel that so many are willing to die for?"

READ OUT

The gospel – so what is it?

Romans 1:1–5 tells us:

- It's God's gospel.
- It's not something new.
- It's all about Jesus.
- It's intended for all.

SO WHAT?

Romans 1:1 states that this is God's gospel. Therefore:

- We need to understand and be able to share it correctly.
- We can be assured of its power.
- We are not responsible for whether or not people become Christians. This is reassuring and takes the pressure off us to make converts.

Romans 1:2 tells us the gospel is not something new. It was promised by the prophets in the Old Testament. Therefore:

- The gospel is rooted in Old Testament prophecy and fulfilled in the life, death and resurrection of Jesus.

Romans 1:3 states that the gospel is all about Jesus. Therefore:

- The focus of our message must be Jesus. For instance, when Wesley preached he used to comment, "I gave them Christ."
- The gospel begins and ends with who Jesus is and what he has done for us, not with what we need or think we want.

Romans 1:4–5 states that the gospel is intended for all. Therefore:

- The gospel is for young, old, male, female and all nationalities.
- The gospel needs to be presented to everyone.

INSTRUCTIONS

- In the next part of the session the group will be required to look up five sets of Bible verses and place them into the appropriate box in their workbooks.
- Divide the group into five and give each one a set of verses to look up.
- Gather the group back together and ask them to comment on their findings.
- As you progress through each slide
    - ask how the verses make people feel, then
    - ask how they are going to get the content of those verses over to their friends.
    - Spend a few moments discussing the implications for both the group and their non-Christian friends.
    - Allow time for discussion.
- Challenge people about this "new life in Christ" – have they grasped this for themselves?

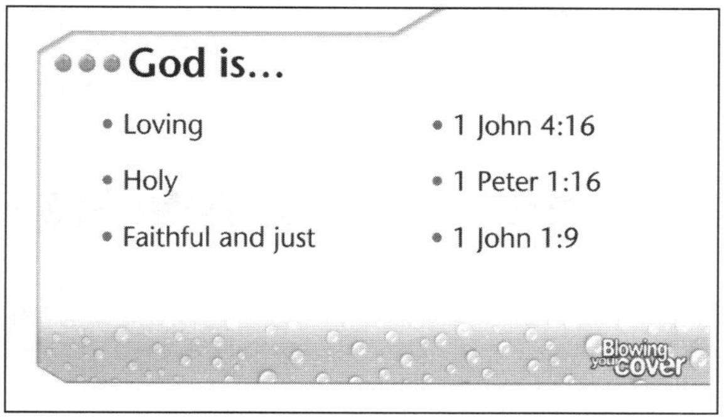

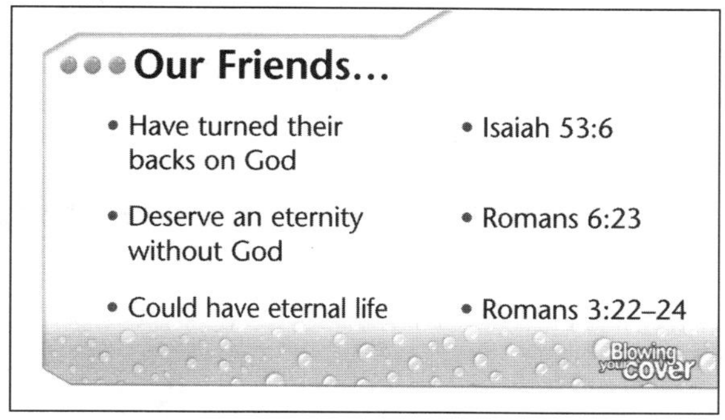

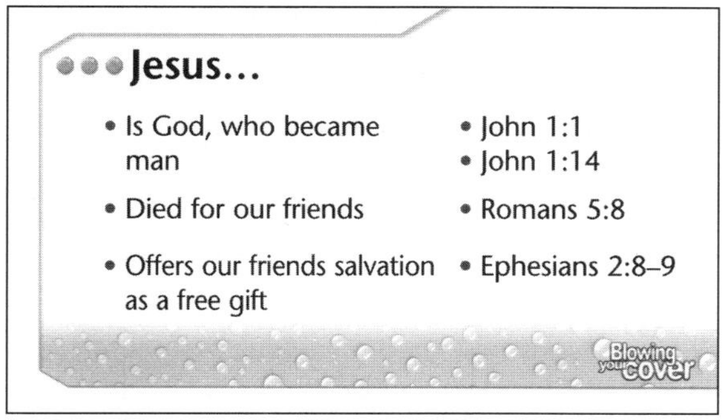

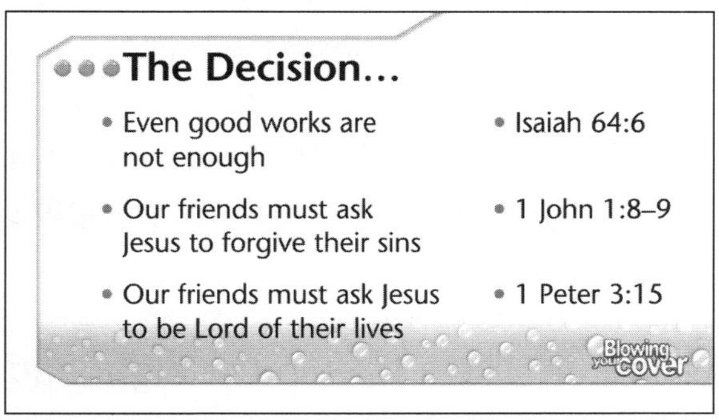

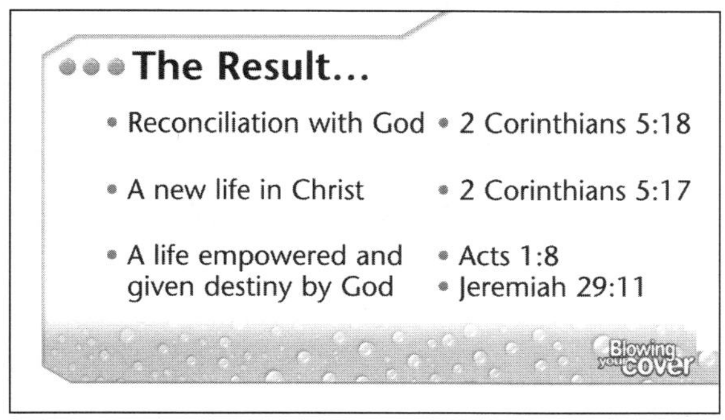

SO WHAT?

It is important that as Christians we grasp this "new life in Christ". John chapter 7 states that is it out of our innermost being that streams of living water flow, and it is this living water that will influence and affect the people within our sphere of influence.

The Great Commission

MEDIA PACK DVD MOOD ENHANCER 1 – DIVINE OPPORTUNITIES

READ OUT

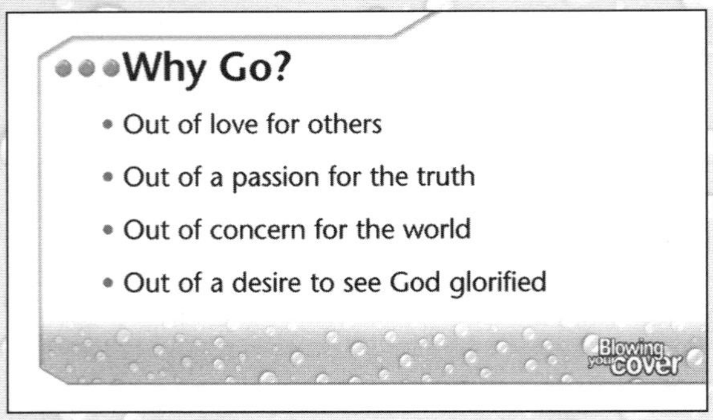

SO WHAT?

- **2 Corinthians 5:14** states that Christ's love should compel us to tell our friends about Jesus. This is a vital aspect of our mission – we MUST love the lost!
- **John 8:32** states that truth sets people free. Remind people that we live in a world with very few absolutes and only Jesus brings absolute truth into people's lives.
- **1 Thessalonians 5:1–3** states that Christ will return like a thief in the night and that many will be unprepared for his return. Remind people that all it takes for evil to prevail is for God's people to do nothing.
- **2 Thessalonians 1:11–12** states that God's name will be lifted up through our lives.

SO WHAT?

Emphasise that it is "as we go" about our everyday lives that we are called to make disciples. Emphasise the making of disciples, not just converts.

INSTRUCTIONS

- Ask the next two questions and give the group time to write down the answers before progressing.
- These questions lead into the "Lifestyle Evangelism" slides that follows.

READ OUT

Write down the role your church plays in evangelism.

SO WHAT?

This question allows people to reflect on what their church is doing in evangelism. Ask people to share their answers with the group. There are no right or wrong answers. "Bolt-on", event-driven evangelism is often referred to at this point. If this occurs, mention that evangelism is about who we are as well as what we do.

Remind people that whilst we can organise evangelistic events, it is not the events that are evangelistic but the Christians at the events.

READ OUT

Write down the role that you play in evangelism.

SO WHAT?

This question allows people to reflect on what role they play in evangelism and begins the thinking process for the following activity.

Open the question up and allow people to discuss their answers.

READ OUT

In the adjacent box draw four circles that represent the rough percentage of your week involved in: family life, work, social activities and evangelism.

SO WHAT?

Some people's circles may overlap or vary in size. The point of this illustration is to challenge a common misconception that evangelism plays only a small part in our lives. Rather, evangelism encompasses everything we do. Progress through the slides to illustrate this.

INSTRUCTIONS

- Ask people to talk about the size of their circles BEFORE you show the second slide. Many will have small social activities circles. This is a common problem that the course aims to address.
- Ask how many people have small social lives. Generally this is the case and therefore we need to be more involved in out-of-church activities, such as clubs, meals, or rediscover forgotten hobbies/interests.

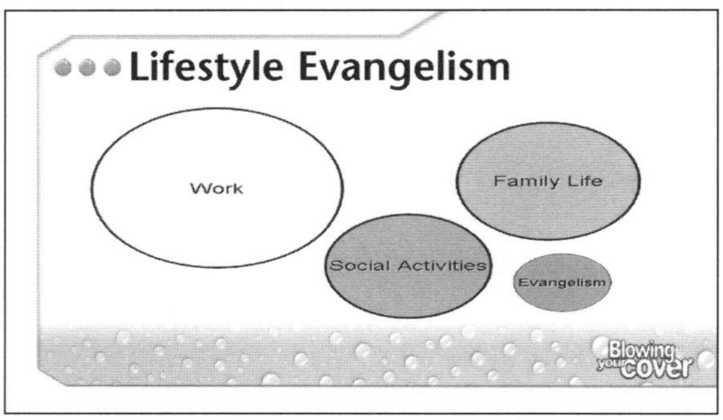

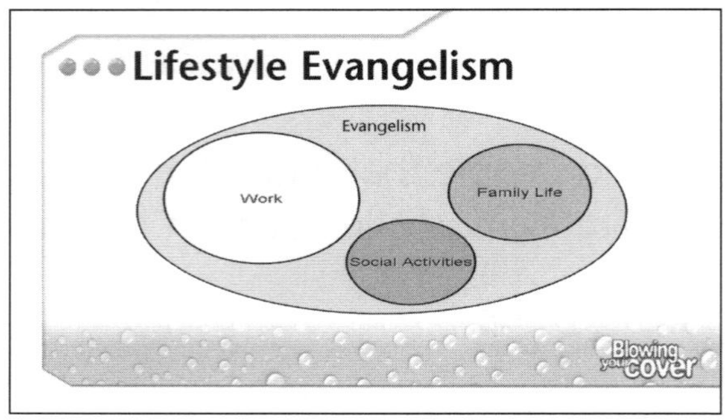

SO WHAT?

The final slide emphasises that ALL we do can be seen as evangelism. This might include picking the children up from school and chatting at the school gate, or going out for the evening with our friends.

These friends are what Blowing Your Cover calls your "sphere of influence".

READ OUT

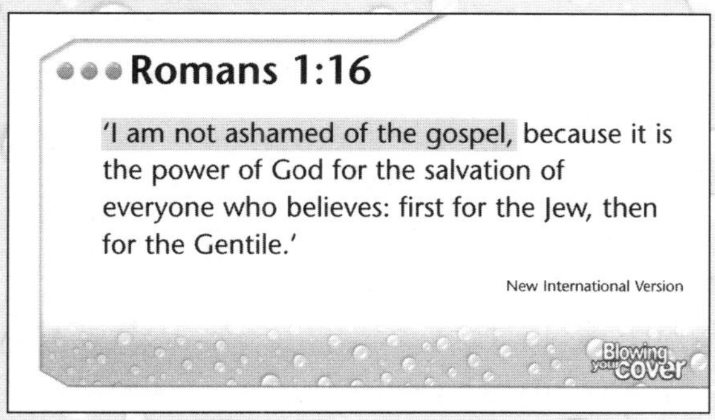

SO WHAT?

Emphasise that we do not need to be ashamed of the gospel or apologise for our faith. We should be willing to share our faith whenever the opportunity occurs.

Presenting the gospel

INSTRUCTIONS

- What follows is a series of diagrams that are designed to equip the members of the group with a means of effectively presenting the gospel in a memorable and graphic form.
- If they already have their own method then they can use whatever they are comfortable with.

READ OUT

1. Begin by drawing a big letter "C" with two ellipses at the top and bottom. In the top one, write the word "God". List some of his characteristics, e.g. holy, eternal, and end with the fact that he is the creator.

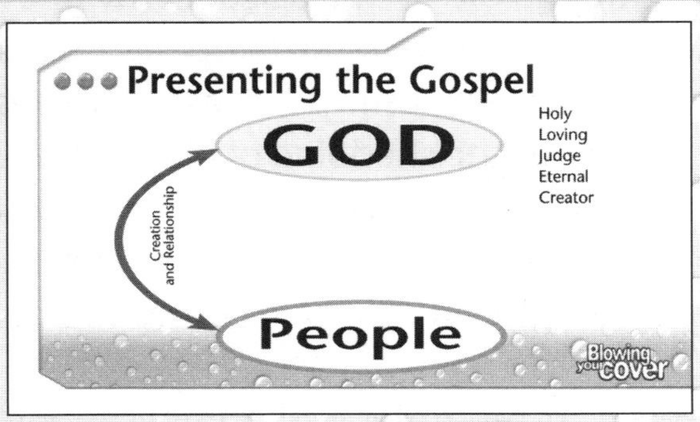

Now write the word "People" in the bottom ellipse, explaining that God and humankind enjoyed a relationship with each other. Lastly, turn the remaining arc into a double-headed arrow and write "Creation & Relationship" along it.

READ OUT

2. Draw a cross over the double-headed arrows and explain that when humankind disobeyed God, sin entered the world, putting a barrier between them. Draw the cloud and list some of the results of sin – being dead to God, physical death and humanity's sinful nature.

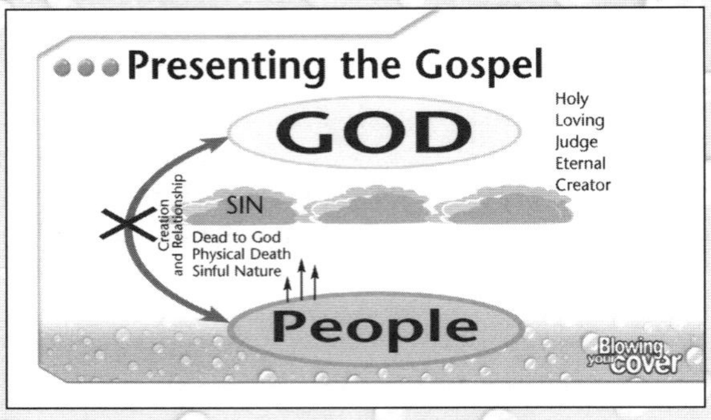

Now draw in the little arrows, which reach up from "People" to "God". Explain that men and women try to find purpose and fulfilment in life through relationships, status or even religion. However, no matter how hard they try, they cannot reach God. Shade in the bottom ellipse to highlight how totally sinful and corrupt humankind is before God.

READ OUT

3. Draw a large arrow from "God" to "People". Explain that God out of his great mercy and love sent his son Jesus into the world.

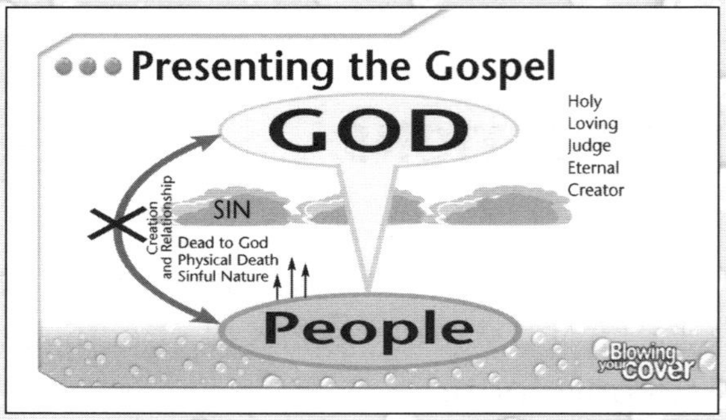

READ OUT

4. Jesus lived an amazing life but came primarily to die in our place. Draw in the cross and explain what happened when Jesus died, using these verses: "…without the shedding of blood there is no forgiveness" (**Hebrews 9:22**) and "Jesus answered, 'I am the way and the truth and the life. No one comes to the Father except through me'" (**John 14:6**).

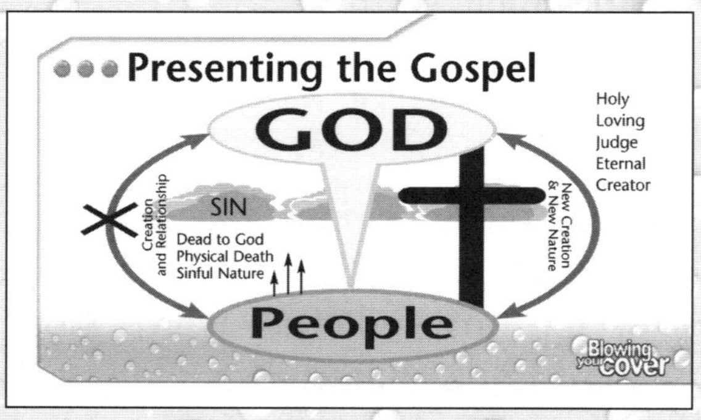

Explain in more detail the implications of the cross, how God's judgement was satisfied. Finally, complete the last part of the missing circle, writing, "New Creation & New Nature" along the arrow. Talk about what it means to be a new creation in Christ, reconciled to God, and to have received a new nature.

SO WHAT?

Learning a graphical method of presenting the gospel is a fantastic way to explain to someone the main points of the gospel. The diagram enhances interaction and allows people time to think through the main points of the gospel.

Taking that vital step

MEDIA PACK DVD MOOD ENHANCER 2 – LIVING GUILT-FREE

READ OUT

Sometimes as we share the gospel, some people will be ready to respond and make a decision to become a Christian. The following are helpful pointers to help you lead those who are ready to make a firm commitment to Christ.

Work together with the Holy Spirit

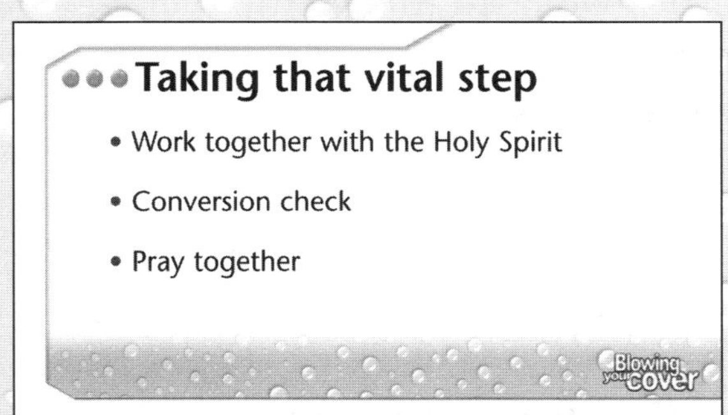

The Holy Spirit has already been working in the life of the person concerned; therefore, we need to co-operate with the Holy Spirit – like a midwife in helping a birth. We can't start or stop it. If they are ready to become a Christian explain that this will be the most exciting step they will ever make. As they take this step the Holy Spirit may also touch delicate issues in their lives – not because He's unjust but because He wants the best for them. Therefore remember to be sensitive.

During the conversation, check that they:

- Believe that Jesus is the Son of God
- Believe that Jesus died on the cross for their sin
- Have come to the point of wanting to become a Christian
- Are ready to let God have Lordship over their lives
- Are ready to accept God's forgiveness

If not, they may still be in the process of thinking issues through.

SO WHAT?

These are the basic essentials of the salvation process that we discussed earlier. If someone is not ready to become a Christian, don't panic; give them time to think things through. Never force someone to become a Christian. We want people to have a genuine encounter with Christ.

READ OUT

Remember

Each individual needs to be ready to make their own decision in their own time.

SO WHAT?

Different people can take more time to think through the implications of the gospel; we need to give them time.

READ OUT

Pray

Pray together. Lead them in a prayer if they are unsure what to say:

- Help them to ask for God's forgiveness.
- Help them to ask for God's leadership from now on in their life.
- Help them to ask for God's power to live a Spirit-filled life.

After the prayer remember:

- Not everyone will react the same. Some people will become emotional and others may not react at all. What matters is that they took a step of faith, not that some specific feeling is evoked.
- An excellent verse to reinforce the step they have just taken is **Luke 15:10**, "... there is rejoicing in the presence of the angels of God over one sinner who repents."

INSTRUCTIONS

- The following list outlines some of the ways we can help a new Christian. Teach the group not to put pressure on people when they first become Christians.
- Emphasise the last two sentences in the "Read Out" box below.

READ OUT

What next?

- Stick with your friend and be prepared to disciple them.
- Go to church meetings and worship God together.
- Help your friend develop Christian friendships, including becoming involved in Alpha, similar enquirer courses or a small group.
- Encourage your friend to pray and read the Bible regularly.
- Encourage your friend to be baptised.
- Encourage your friend to maintain their existing friendships where possible.
- Teach them who they are in Christ.

All these changes will not happen at once so don't overwhelm your friend. They are produced by the work of the Holy Spirit and it is not for us to try to force people into a certain mould.

SO WHAT?

Remind the group that this is the work of the Holy Spirit. Our role is to encourage and support.

READ OUT

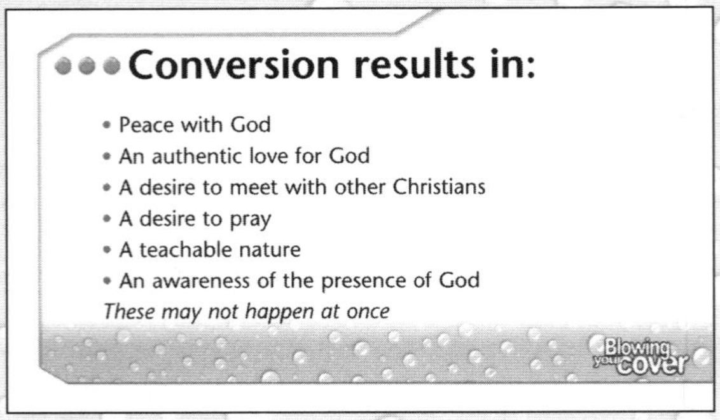

INSTRUCTIONS

- Place a big emphasis on the "Important" statement. Ask how many people were followed up when they became Christians.
- **We cannot change the past but we can change the future. (See Philippians 3:13–14.)**

READ OUT

Important

Commit yourself to making sure you or someone else looks after these new Christians. Discipleship is vital, as we need to give these new Christians a firm foundation on which to build their new lives.

DISCUSSION

INSTRUCTIONS

- Allow ten minutes for this and make sure you participate in this exercise too.
- Work through the two discussions, one after the other. Some group members may want to take the opportunity to practise sharing the gospel using the diagrams used earlier in the session.
- Pair up with a different member of the group for each one. When you gather people back together, ask one or two to share what they learnt. Remember, it is only a workshop and real life can be different, but it is a very helpful exercise.

READ OUT

Jim works in your office and you have been praying for him for three months. This is the third time you have had lunch together. At lunch you ask Jim if you can briefly explain what it means to be a Christian. Jim is extremely interested in the gospel and ready to become a Christian.

READ OUT

Two of you are visiting Jane, a single mother whose son attends the "Kidz Club" that your church runs. You visit her house every week to call on her son. Two months ago in response to her ill health, you had the opportunity to pray for physical healing. On arriving she pours out her heart to you. She says she is not able to cope with life and asks for help.

Key Scripture

- **Romans 3:23–24.**

MEDIA PACK DVD SESSION ONE – CLOSURE

Blowing your cover

Session 2

Your Sphere of Influence

Pre-Session Notes

- The approximate time required for this session is one and a half hours, depending on the amount of time spent in group interaction.
- Make sure you are familiar with the accompanying Media Pack by watching all the session 2 media clips..
- Make sure that you complete the Blowing Your Cover questionnaire prior to the session. Ensure you make people aware that total table answers are not sequential.
- People may need time to reflect and pray about the two people they would like to include on the Friendship List. If this is the case don't hurry them.
- Print off the respective number of "Evangelism Style" forms (found on the DVD), depending on the number of groups to be trained. These should be distributed to the group leaders at the commencement of the session.
- Why not show the prayer clip from the media pack at the next prayer meeting.

Welcome

START MEDIA PACK DVD SESSION TWO – WELCOME

READ OUT

AIMS

1. To start your Friendship List by prayerfully selecting people from your sphere of influence
2. To know your two strongest evangelism styles
3. To recognise the evangelism styles of other people in your group

INSTRUCTIONS

- Have the members of the group quote the Bible verse from the previous session to each other and write it in the space provided in their workbooks. Then reveal the answer using the slide.

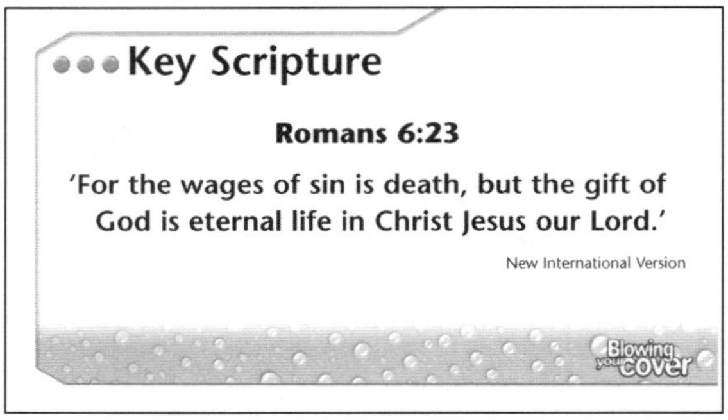

- Ask if anybody would like to talk about how God has used them since the last session.
- Encourage people to be open and honest.

Understanding our friends

- The first task is to write, in the circles provided, the names of five *non-Christian* friends that people spend time with.
- Some Christians may struggle to find five. It is vital that we do not make people feel guilty for not having many non-Christian friends but encourage people to write down as many as they can.

SO WHAT?

Later on in this session people will choose two of these names for their Friendship List; they should be friends.

INSTRUCTIONS

- Now introduce the next slide: two typical friends. They represent typical people in society today.

- Remind people that these people are representative of their friends, and that any of the following points could relate to them.

READ OUT

Meet a typical friend:

- They may have rejected the idea of going to church, but they have not rejected the idea of God.

- Even though they have few absolute morals, they secretly want them for themselves and for their children if they have any.

- If questioned they do not really know what they believe.

- They may actually try going to church if someone asks them.

- They will ditch your friendship if they think they are your project and not your friend.

- They want to know and experience something.

- They are probably more willing to talk about God than you think and may well want you to start the conversation.

As your friends receive answers to some of their questions, they move closer to being more interested in Jesus and Christianity.

INSTRUCTIONS

- Ask the group, "Do any of the above points describe your friends?"
- Allow people to discuss any issues this raises.

SO WHAT?

There are lots of issues mentioned above but a point to highlight is "treating people as a project". This completely defeats the idea of being a friend, yet many Christians do this.

It is important that we are friends with people even if they reject Christianity. Note how people react to this statement. It is vital that this point is understood.

Moving our friends along

INSTRUCTIONS

- Here we introduce the "Disbeliever" to "New Believer" scale. Our non-Christian friends fall into one of four categories.

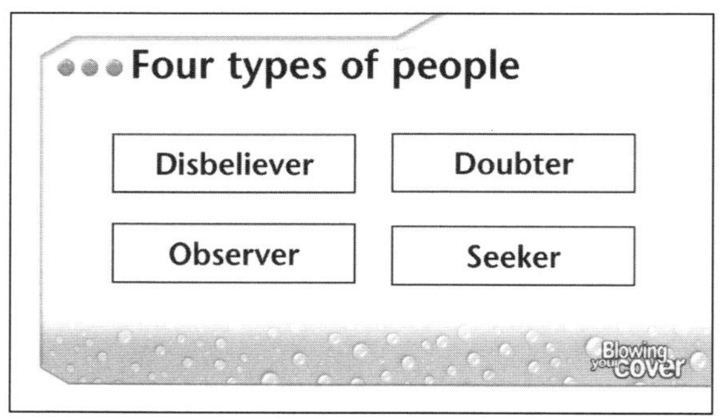

READ OUT

Your friend's interest in Christianity tends to fall into one of the following categories:

- Disbeliever, Doubter, Observer or Seeker

INSTRUCTIONS

- Move to the next slide.

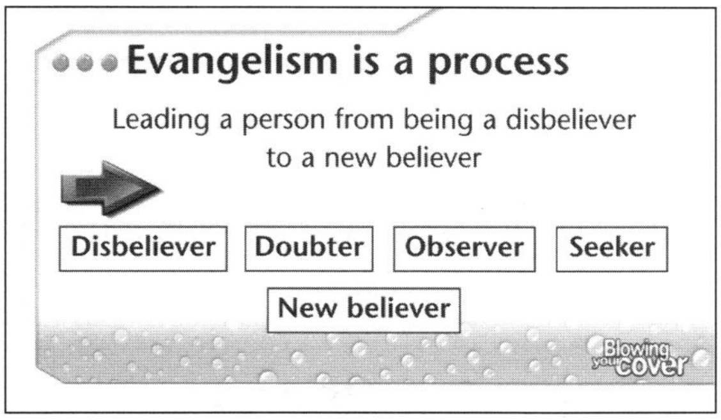

- Use **1 Corinthians 3:6**. It says, "I planted the seed, Apollos watered it, but God made it grow." Then mention that although we are not all called to be evangelists, each one of us plays a vital part in other people's spiritual journey. For instance, every time we share our faith with people we act as a single link in a long chain.

READ OUT

Important

Evangelism is a process – it involves moving a person from their location on the scale to becoming a New Believer. (We are not labelling people here, rather helping ourselves to understand where our friends might be on their journey.)

INSTRUCTIONS

- A description of the four categories follows. There are some hints and tips in how to engage these different types of people.

- Talk around the following scale and encourage discussion.

- Read through the details of one of the non-Christian categories and encourage the group to read through the details of the others at a later stage.

Scale	Disbeliever	Doubter
Description	They do not believe in a supreme being and are cynical about Christianity.	They are not sure Christianity is true. They are sceptical about it.
Hints & Tips	Live a Christian life in front of these people.	Tell them how real Jesus is to you.

Scale	Observer	Seeker
Description	They do not see an immediate need to believe in Christ, but are willing to examine any claims that are made.	They are willing to talk about the relevance of the gospel.
Hints & Tips	Ask them questions concerning eternal issues and provide them with relevant reading materials.	Take the initiative to share the gospel or invite them to an Alpha or similar enquirer's course.

Scale	New Believer
Description	They display the fruits of repentance and faith. They are new disciples, willing to be integrated into the church and continuing to grow in character, lifestyle and service.
IMPORTANT	Someone needs to support and disciple them.

INSTRUCTIONS

- At this point ask the group to write down the names that they listed in the circles.
- Now ask them to put them into a category: Disbeliever, Doubter, Observer or Seeker.
- Some people may not fall neatly into one category. These are simply guidelines to help us visualise where our friends are on their spiritual journey.

Introducing the Friendship List

- In this section we start to create a Friendship List for every individual in the group. Initially everyone will begin with two names.

- Move to the next slide and give people time to complete this task. At this stage not everyone will be clear on who the two people should be. Remind the group that for now it is best to only pencil in these names.

READ OUT

From the five people above, write down in the space below the names of two friends you would like to see become Christians:

The way it will work:

- Your Friendship List – two people you meet with and pray for on a regular basis.

- Your small-group's Friendship List – the combined number of names from everyone in the small-group. The group is encouraged to pray for these people on a regular basis.

READ OUT

Remember

Friendships can be difficult to maintain at times. However, we need to show the love of God and develop friendships that last, regardless of whether or not people agree with the Christian message.

SO WHAT?

This is an important point. We cannot walk away from our friends simply because they do not agree with our message.

DISCUSSION

INSTRUCTIONS

- There follows three scenarios for discussion. Work through the first two and allow the group time to think and write out their answers in the space provided. The third discussion takes place in the form of a Mood Enhancer.
- When they have completed the exercise, ask, "Would you bring Christianity into the conversation or would you feel too embarrassed?"
- Allow time for discussion.

READ OUT

Situation One

You are with a non-Christian friend walking in the country; all around you there is beauty, spectacular scenery and the wonders of creation...

What do you say or do?

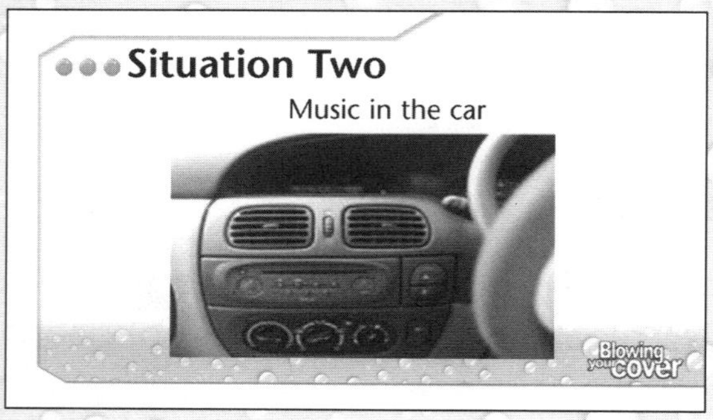

Situation Two

Your non-Christian friend switches on the CD player in your car and worship music starts playing...

What do you say or do?

INSTRUCTIONS

- Move to the next slide and read out the quote from Steve Hill before moving on to the third scenario. (Steve Hill is the evangelist who led the Pensacola Revival, 1996–1999.)

READ OUT

> **Divine Appointments**
>
> 'I don't expect you to tell everyone you meet day in and day out that you are a Christian but I do expect you to say something when God obviously opens the door.'
>
> Steve Hill, Pensacola 1998
>
> Blowing your cover

SO WHAT?

We often ask God to give us "opportunities" to share our faith and then fail to seize the moment! Encourage the group to be bold because divine appointments come our way all the time, give an example of one in your life.

Situation Three

MEDIA PACK DVD MOOD ENHANCER 1 – STITCHED UP BY GOD

Sharing your faith

INSTRUCTIONS

- This section helps the group to think about how effective they are in sharing their faith. Ask, "Do you draw people to the gospel or turn people away?"
- The next set of notes provides you with help on how we set about sharing the gospel.
- You may want to refer to John chapter 4. This illustrates how Jesus talked to a woman at a well. Note that he communicated in a natural and personal way. He did not use "evangelistic techniques". He simply became her friend.

READ OUT

What must it be?

- Natural
- Personal

How is it achieved?

- Verbally
- Gradually
- By being empowered by the Holy Spirit

What effect does this have on us?

- We should be "salt and light"
- We become "living letters"

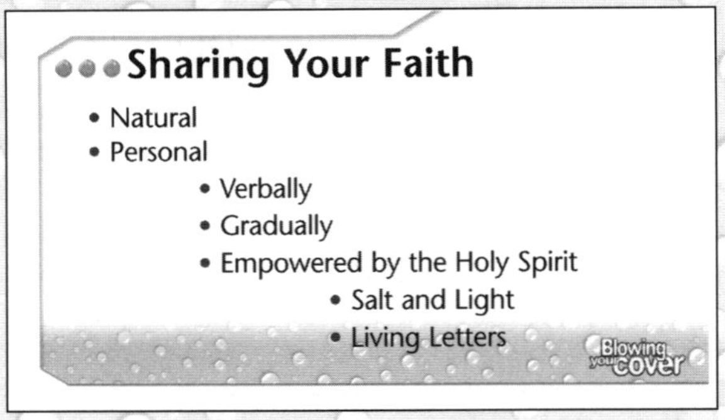

SO WHAT?

Natural

We can often fall into the trap of thinking we are "going to witness" when actually it should be what comes naturally to us.

Personal

Because our evangelism should be natural, it will therefore be personal. Non-Christians, in a post-modern society, have little time for "hit and run" evangelism.

Verbally

Many people say actions speak louder than words. **Romans 10:17** states, "Consequently, faith comes from hearing the message, and the message is heard through the word of Christ."

Gradually

People need to hear the gospel and think it through before making a decision.

Empowered by the Holy Spirit

Acts 11:24 states, "He (Barnabas) was a good man, full of the Holy Spirit and faith, and a great number of people were brought to the Lord."

Salt and light/Living Letters

- Being salt and light allows us to influence and make a difference to the people around us. **Matthew 5:13** states, "You are the salt of the earth."
- In **2 Corinthians 3:2** Paul talks about Christians being living letters that people "read". Remember, people observe how we live.
- Francis of Assisi once said: "I witness to people wherever I go and sometimes I use words." You may want to allow people to discuss the implications of this statement.

READ OUT

Important

We are all different! You do not have to be a famous evangelist. God wants to use you. Remember, he wants you to be yourself.

YOU ARE UNIQUE!

MEDIA PACK DVD MOOD ENHANCER 2 – YOU ARE UNIQUE

Blowing Your Cover questionnaire

INSTRUCTIONS

- Give the group up to fifteen minutes to complete the questionnaire.

- Encourage people not to spend too long thinking about each question; we are looking for a "gut instinct" rather than a theological reflection on their lives.

Questionnaire

Record your response to each of the 40 statements according to whether you think the statement applies to you:

- 0 – Not at all
- 1 – Rarely
- 2 – Often
- 3 – Always

Blowing your cover

- Once everyone has completed it they will need to add up their scores by transferring them onto the total table in the Workbooks. *The total table answer numbers in the workbook are not sequential.*

- Now ask the group to note their two highest scores in the box provided in their Workbook. Some people have two equal scores. In this case note both of them.

SO WHAT?

- Evangelism styles flow out of who we are in Christ and the personality that God has given us. Remind people that we don't have to try to be someone we are not.

- You may find that some people have four scores that are close together. If this is the case encourage them; this is very positive and it means that they can be "all things to all people" and adapt easily to different people's personalities.

Blowing Your Cover evangelism styles

INSTRUCTIONS

- In the Workbook detailed notes about four evangelism styles are now given: Direct, Personal, Thinker and Helper.

Evangelism Styles

Each has its own distinctive traits, strengths and areas that require development:

Direct	Personal
Thinker	Helper

Blowing your cover

- Ask the group to read the pages that relate to their two highest scores. Watch their reactions as they do this. People are often surprised when they identify their personal evangelism style.
- Progress through the slide; show each of the four styles in order. Spend some time discussing the evangelistic opportunities for each style and encourage people to think through what additional opportunities each style could have.
- Ask for a show of hands for each of the four styles and record how many Direct, Personal, Thinker and Helper people there are. Obviously, the two largest categories represent the dominant evangelism styles for your church. Encourage the church to work evangelistically in these main styles but stress that the other styles need to be incorporated as well.
- Have them make a note in their Workbooks of other people's evangelistic styles. Mention that people can work together using complementary styles as they reach out to their non-Christian friends. Who will their friends get on well with? Ask the group to give one or two examples of how people with different evangelistic styles could work together.
- It is helpful for group leaders to make a note of this too. Use the "Evangelism Style" form provided.

READ OUT

Who in your small-group has a style that would get on well with the people on your Friendship List?

Important

Knowing your style will help you and your small-group to be more effective in sharing your faith with others.

Key Scripture

- **Romans 6:23.**

MEDIA PACK DVD SESSION TWO – CLOSURE

Blowing your cover

Session 3

Connecting with Your Culture

Pre-Session Notes

- The approximate time required for this session is one and a half hours, depending on the amount of time spent in group interaction.
- Make sure you are familiar with the accompanying Media Pack by watching all the session 3 media clips..
- Read through the additional notes (at the end of this session) entitled "A Cultural Overview of Western Society" in order to facilitate a discussion on this topic during the first part of this session.
- Watch the Mark Greene, London Institute for Contempory Christianity (LICC) Session from the Leader's Guide DVD.
- Allow adequate time for people to think through and pray about adding a third name to their Friendship List.

Welcome

START MEDIA PACK DVD SESSION THREE – WELCOME

READ OUT

AIMS

1. To gain an understanding of our culture.
2. To add a third person to your Friendship List.
3. To examine culture-connecting qualities.

INSTRUCTIONS

- Have the members of the group quote the Bible verse from the previous session to each other and write it in the space provided in their Workbooks. Then reveal the answer using the slide.

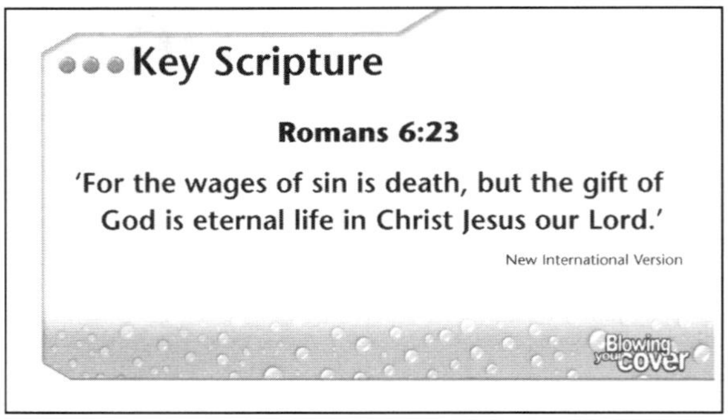

- Ask if anybody would like to talk about how God has used them since the last session.
- Encourage people to be open and honest.

Understanding our culture

INSTRUCTIONS

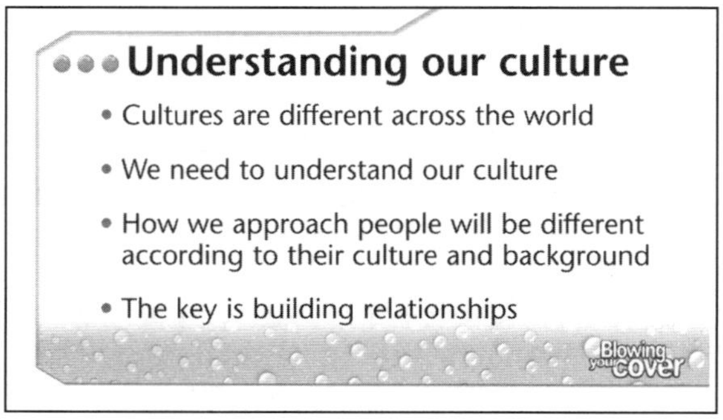

- Allow 30 minutes for this section.
- Use the enclosed additional notes at the end of this session to aid the participants' understanding of the

culture they live in. Each Workbook also has the same set of notes for further reading.

- As the leader you will need to grasp these concepts and expand some aspects to promote discussion. To assist you, watch the LICC Culture Session from the Leader's DVD. This will enhance your understanding of the topic.

- There are no right or wrong answers here; we simply want people to begin to grasp some of the issues that the current culture poses to them as they share their faith.

- As well as the "Ask Yourself" questions in the cultural notes, consider the following questions:

    - "Are we connecting with our culture?"

    - "How do non-Christians perceive the church?"

    - "Do we actually listen to our non-Christian friends?"

READ OUT

Cultures are different across the world. These differences can occur both within a country and in a local area; therefore, understanding our target culture(s) is essential. For instance, in the UK we have moved from modern culture to post-modern culture.

In our desire to reach the people on our Friendship List we need to understand their background/culture.

Reaching someone with a Christian background is different from reaching a person from a secular background or from a different ethnic group. The apostle Paul used a different initial approach in Athens from the one he used in Jerusalem. Whatever culture we are living in or trying to reach, the universal key, as Paul shows, is to build relationships. Over time and through friendship, we can demonstrate and communicate the gospel. As we spend time with people we gradually and continually expose them to the gospel. This "drip, drip" approach can leave our friends thirsty for more and should not alienate them.

SO WHAT?

This has a huge impact on how we share our faith with our friends. Some of our friends will have a "modern" outlook on life, some will have a "post-modern" outlook and some will have a mixture of the two.

It's all about people

INSTRUCTIONS

In this section point out the following and allow time for discussion.

- We are not salesmen; we have "life-changing news"
- We must never impose Christianity on people

READ OUT

As we engage in evangelism, we should never become "salesmen" for the gospel, simply transmitting data to those who "buy" our product. Instead, we must realise that the gospel involves loving people and building relationships.

If our view of evangelism is simply to get others to agree that four or five thoughts about Christianity are correct, pray a prayer, and then go to heaven when they die, then we are missing a vital element. We are called to make disciples; therefore, our task is to bring those on our Friendship List into a twofold relationship. The first relationship is that of coming to know God personally, living for him and enjoying him both now and for ever. The second is to help these people become rooted into the house of God, where they can grow in their newfound faith.

Winning others to Christ and making disciples is all about connecting with our culture and building those all-important relationships.

INSTRUCTIONS

- Move to the next slide and read out the two questions. Instruct the group to write their answers to each question in the space provided in the Workbook. Allow time for discussion.

READ OUT

INSTRUCTIONS

- Instruct the group to look up **Acts 8:4–8** and answer the question, "What is the difference between an evangelist and someone who shares their faith on a regular basis?"
- Ask the group to write their answers in the space provided in the workbook, and then allow time for discussion.

SO WHAT?

Point out that we are *all* called to share our faith, not just the evangelists. In the New Testament the normal Christian life was for everybody to share their faith.

We need to be relational people who build genuine friendships with non-Christians. We also need to be people who become less introspective and more outward-looking.

READ OUT

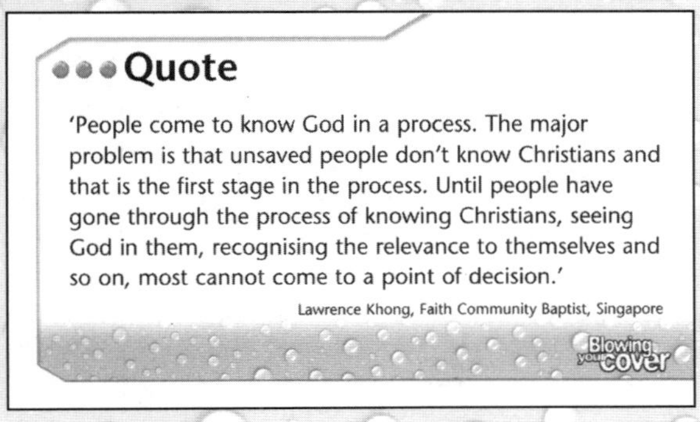

Take a break

MEDIA PACK DVD MOOD ENHANCER 1 – TAKE A BREAK

READ OUT

It's easy to look at evangelism as being something that only trained specialists get involved in, or to feel that evangelism only happens when a few enthusiasts make a sortie to the High Street to talk to strangers. There is a need for full-time evangelists and street outreach, but networking is something that EVERYONE is involved in. Blowing Your Cover calls this "your sphere of influence".

Adding a third name to your Friendship List

INSTRUCTIONS

With this slide as a background highlight:

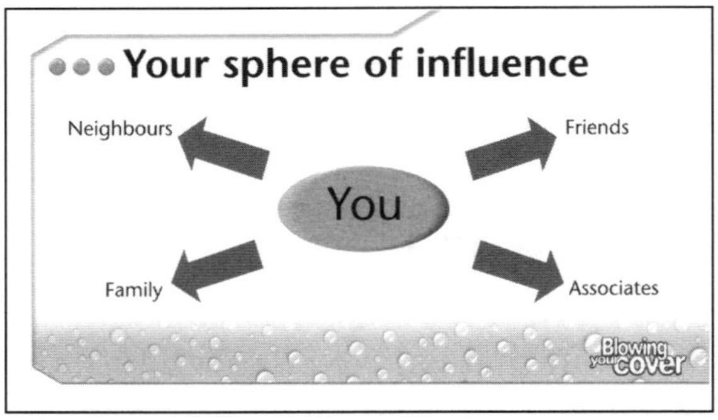

- Evangelism is not a bolt-on option to the church.
- We all have a network of friends, people who are within our sphere of influence and some of them may well be interested in the gospel.

READ OUT

Everybody has people they meet regularly, namely **family**, **friends**, **neighbours** (people living nearby) **and associates** (at work, or an educational institution, for example). You don't have to start up "cold" conversations with these people, because the foundations of relationships have already been laid.

Friendships will demand patience, creativity, possibly being a "servant" and a definite commitment to the long haul. As we build relationships and show love to the people God brings into our lives, then Disbelievers, Doubters and Observers can become Seekers. In time, we will also have the joy of seeing some of them being saved and added into God's family. God wants to use you to connect with your culture and to see people who are on your Friendship List added to his church.

READ OUT

Acts 2:47

"And the Lord added to their number daily those who were being saved."

INSTRUCTIONS

- Instruct the group to take a few minutes to complete the table in their Workbooks. They do not have to complete every single space provided.

Quote

'You can make more friends in two months by being interested in other people than you can in two years by trying to get people interested in you.'

Dale Carnegie, 'How to win friends and influence people'

- Then instruct them to prayerfully select one of the above people and add them to their Friendship List from Session Two. They should now have three names on their Friendship List.

- Remind the group that in order to develop strong friendships we need to take a real interest in our friends. We need to support them and not make a project out of them.

SO WHAT?

The group may be surprised at how many people they know, and therefore how many opportunities they have to share the gospel through words and deeds.

Culture-Connecting Qualities

MEDIA PACK DVD MOOD ENHANCER 2 – OFF-FENCE-IVE EVANGELISM

INSTRUCTIONS

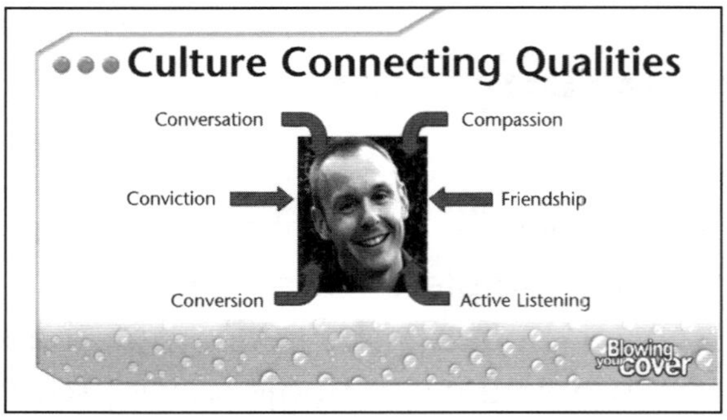

- Now introduce culture-connecting qualities. These are qualities that will help us to break through the worldly façade and make an impact on those around you.
- Compassion, friendship, active listening and conversation are addressed first, then the presentation moves on to the "bridge of friendship", returning to the same slide to complete the conviction and conversion topics.

READ OUT

Remember the friends we talked about in Session Two – our desire is for some of them to become Christians and to be introduced to God's family: the church. Yet these friends are immersed within the current culture. In order to reach them with the gospel message it is helpful to think about six culture-connecting qualities that as Christians we need to develop and display.

READ OUT

1. Compassion not duty

This is where it all starts. God's compassion is revealed to us through the life, death and resurrection of Christ. We see the same compassion demonstrated within the life of Christ; for instance, we read in **Mark 1:41**, "Filled with compassion, Jesus reached out his hand and touched the man..." As we are disciples of Christ we too should desire this compassion.

The very nature of compassion is all about being, not just doing. Quite often out of duty we feel obliged to be there for our friends, when the real response should flow out of unconditional love. Very often we are encouraged to pastor our Christian friends, which is admirable, but we also need to pastor our non-Christian friends as well.

Compassion, then, should flow out of our very innermost being, as an overflow of our life in Christ and our desire to be like him.

INSTRUCTIONS

- Spend a few minutes praying for each other, asking God to impart to us his love and compassion for our friends.

READ OUT

2. Friendship not projects

We often hear Christians use certain words in connection with their friends, such as "befriend" and "contact". For example, "He is on my contact list" or "I intend to befriend her to encourage her to come to church!" Whilst their intentions are good, the very nature of the thinking behind these comments conveys a sense of making your friend a project.

Friendships are valuable and we need to grow and develop them with the help of God. A good friendship is based on trust and achieved over a period of time. It is not something that can be rushed. Sometimes we can go out of our way to try and "meet new friends" when actually they are closer than we think.

Some people meet their friends in the workplace; for others it may be the club, school or college. Wherever you meet your friends, make sure you take time out to spend with them, enjoy their company and take an interest in them.

INSTRUCTIONS

- Instruct the group to spend a few minutes thinking about their friends and how they view friendship. Allow discussion if time allows.

READ OUT

3. Active listening not prejudgement

Listening is not the same as hearing. Often people hear but they don't actively listen to what their friends are saying. We need to be people who actively listen to the words of our friends, both spoken and unspoken.

Active listening is a way of listening and responding to your friends that improves understanding. When people talk to each other, they don't always listen attentively. They can easily be distracted, are half listening, or they are thinking about something else. When people are sharing their faith, they are often busy formulating a response to what is being said. They assume that they have heard what their friend is saying, so rather than paying attention, they focus on how they can respond to win the argument.

Remember, we are not sharing our faith to win an argument, but to demonstrate the love of Christ. Sadly, we can end up prejudging people by jumping to a conclusion without first hearing and actively listening to what they are really saying.

INSTRUCTIONS

- Challenge the group to practise their listening skills with their friends and report back next week.

READ OUT

4. Conversation not Christian monologue

Conversation by definition is a two-way street and follows on from active listening. It involves taking the time to ask your friends open questions – questions that will open up the conversation further to allow you to explore more about their lives and for them to ask more about your life.

However, as we have just learnt, we need to listen to the answers. After a conversation has been started it is important to be aware of the direction the conversation is taking and how the other person is responding. Based on that assessment, make a decision on whether to continue the conversation or move to a different topic. It is important we do not simply "download" onto our friends and end up with nothing more than a Christian monologue.

Be prepared, though, to enter into a full-length conversation about Christ when the opportunity arises. However, also be prepared to tell them only part of the story and leave them asking for more! The possibilities are endless and exciting!

Below are some questions designed to open up conversation and encourage active listening:

- Why do you think people prefer to live as if God does not exist?
- How do you teach your children right from wrong?
- If you could have God change one thing in your life, what would it be?
- What are your views regarding life after death?
- In your opinion how does someone become a Christian?
- How are you looking for happiness in this life?
- Does your worldview allow for any absolutes?

INSTRUCTIONS

- When we consider sharing our faith with our friends we need to be careful and considerate not to appear pushy and come across as "Bible bashers".
- What follows is a set of four slides designed to illustrate this point.
- Talk around the points as they are presented.

READ OUT

In the first picture we see the basic state of affairs. In this situation there exists a bridge of friendship that will support a maximum load of ten tonnes.

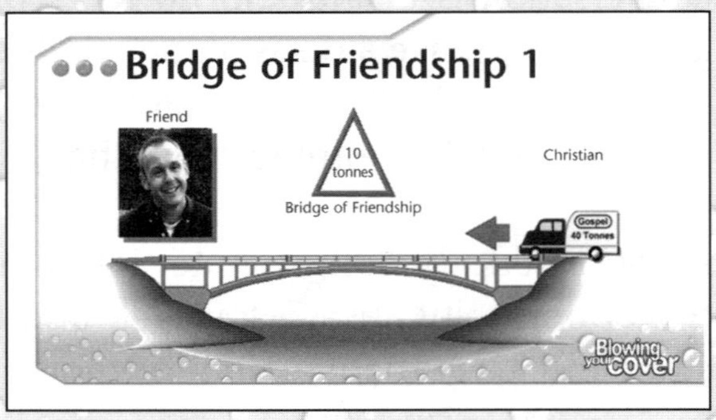

In the second picture what this Christian is trying to accomplish, in one encounter, is to drive the whole gospel over the bridge of friendship. In this illustration a 40-tonne lorry represents this attempt.

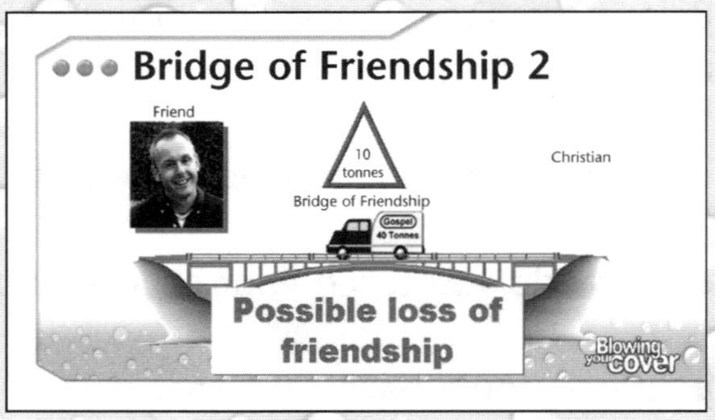

Of course, it does not take a genius to know that this approach is doomed to fail, as the bridge will collapse under the weight. In some cases the bridge of friendship is permanently broken as the non-Christian can think we are just out to "Bible bash" them.

This can be easily avoided. Instead of trying to communicate the whole gospel at one sitting, you can break it down into smaller and more manageable portions that will not cause the bridge of friendship to collapse.

In reality, this means praying and working away over a period of time, possibly strengthening the bridge of friendship, so it can support heavier loads. As has been said earlier, we can gauge how strong the bridge is by observing people's

reactions. Listen out for the telltale sounds of the bridge of friendship creaki
under the strain.

As we spend time with our friends, showing love and genuine concern, this should create a foundation stone where trust and respect can flourish. Arising out of this will come many opportunities to share your faith. Some Christians miss this and their friendship ends in disaster.

If you continue to be patient, bold and wise you will eventually have the opportunity to communicate the whole gospel with many of your friends. The bridge of friendship remains intact, possibly even stronger than it was at first.

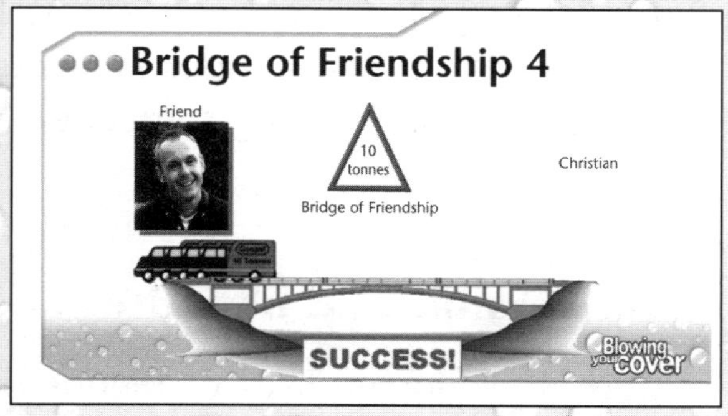

INSTRUCTIONS

- Move on to the next slide.

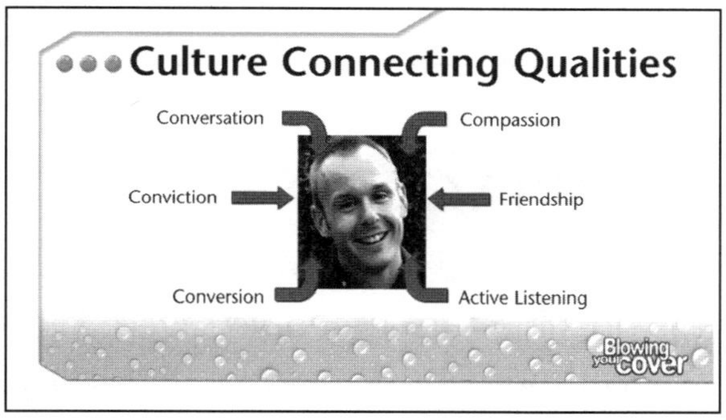

READ OUT

5. Conviction not condemnation

Our friends are on a spiritual journey and as we keep walking with them we are able to demonstrate the love and truths of God through our lives. Be confident that the Holy Spirit will start to convict some of them just as he did with you. Remember it is his job to convict, not ours. We should not condemn our friends but allow them to come to Christ in their way and in their time.

Matthew 7:1–2 says, "Do not judge, or you too will be judged. For in the same way as you judge others, you will be judged, and with the measure you use, it will be measured to you."

As your friendship grows, you will have many opportunities to share the gospel. Therefore, continue to pray that the Holy Spirit will convict your friends of their spiritual condition.

SO WHAT?

It is the Holy Spirit who convicts; it is not our job. Sometimes we want people "whiter than white" before they enter our churches. This should not be the case. Jesus was a friend of sinners.

1 Peter 3:15 says that we should always be prepared to give an answer for the hope that we have. This means thinking through our faith and attempting to answer the difficult questions, or asking someone else to help answer them.

READ OUT

6. Conversion and new life

As God works in the lives of friends on your Friendship List, you will have the opportunity of leading some of them to Christ. Let's look at three examples of conversion.

SO WHAT?

It is possible to see people saved. We are all examples of this. Once each one of us was without Christ; now we are living in Christ. If this can happen for us, why not our friends?

INSTRUCTIONS

- Have the group look at **Luke 19:1–10** and ask them to write their answers in the spaces provided in their Workbook.
- Do the same for **Acts 16:13–15** and **Acts 2:37–46**.

READ OUT

Action point

How would you evaluate where you are in terms of how you are relating to your friends on your Friendship List? Are there areas of strengthening or specific action that you need to take and pray about?

Use the table below to write down the names of your friends and then how well you excel in the culture-connecting qualities. Think through an action plan to help you take the next step with your friends.

Key Scripture

- **Romans 5:8.**

MEDIA PACK DVD SESSION THREE – CLOSURE

Additional Material
A Cultural Overview of Western Society

Starting notes

- In Western culture "modern" refers to a period of time, not to the idea of being "technologically up to date".

- In the Workbook we have only written a short paragraph about different cultures. These extra notes will help you understand the concepts of "pre-modern", "modern" and "post-modern" cultures. Disbelievers, Doubters, Observers and Seekers on your Friendship Lists are profoundly influenced by culture. Through these additional notes you will be able to discover how the Western worldview has developed, where you fit into this worldview and also where your friends fit into it.

- Further reading:

  - Nick Pollard, *Evangelism Made Slightly Less Difficult*, IVP

  - Michael Green, *Critical Choices*, Hodder & Stoughton

  - Nick Spencer, *Beyond Belief*, LICC Publications

  - Mark GreeneΔ, *Imagine* DVD, LICC Publications, UK only

  - All resources can be purchased through our online store: www.blowingyourcover.com

- The six Blowing Your Cover principles relating to culture outlined in these notes are:

  - Principle One: Pre-modern thought

  - Principle Two: Modern thought

  - Principle Three: Post-modern thought

  - Principle Four: Western worldview

  - Principle Five: Christian worldview

  - Principle Six: Imposition?

Principle One: Pre-modern thought

In "pre-modern" times (up to about 1600) people viewed humanity and the world around them as God's creation. When they wanted to discover the truth, they turned to the church. There was a strong belief in sacred texts, such as the Bible, and a strong community life. However, as many people were illiterate this led to "prescribed thought".

Pre-modern viewpoints

Small narrative
A narrative is a worldview, the picture that people have of their world. In pre-modern times this was a small, local viewpoint. People did not travel far and everything they needed was provided in the village area.

Providence
Providence was almost fatalistic and lay in the hands of God. Due to the level of illiteracy, people's view of providence was governed by what they heard from the church. Providence was therefore seen as God's will being applied to daily life.

One truth
The worldview at the time was small, therefore the only accepted truth was the one supplied by the church. There was very little influence from other religions and therefore what was relevant to one person was consequently relevant to the whole village.

Pre-critical
Within this era people did not question beliefs, motives or authority. Many things were taken for granted without being thought through.

Representative building
A building that would typify this period would be Cologne Cathedral. Work began in 1247 and took over 600 years to complete. It was built for the glory of God, points to heaven and was used for worship.

Principle Two: Modern thought

In "modern" times (1600–1960) people's views started to change, primarily because of the French Renaissance and the influence of Descartes whose main work was published in 1637. He is described as the father of modern thought and coined the phrase "I think therefore I am". Society was characterised by reason and rationality (what can be proved to be certain). This resulted in a subtle shift to throw out sacred texts and inhibit the display of emotions (e.g. in the Victorian period this led to the British "stiff upper lip"). Science declared that it would provide all the answers by proof and certainty. This period of time was described as "The Enlightenment". During this period, with the advent of the printing press, people became increasingly more literate.

Modern viewpoints

Meta-narrative

In the modern era a "bigger picture" worldview has increasingly developed. As travel increases, so people's concepts and beliefs are challenged. People are aware of other faiths but remain faithful to their heritage.

Cause and effect

With the advance of science, people begin to question the simple ideas of providence. They push the boundaries and discover cause and effect. This makes a huge impact on society. Darwin's theory of evolution promotes cause and effect, which subtly erodes the meta-narrative of Christianity in society.

Method

Truth in a modern society can only be accepted if it can be proved. Science refines new ideas and subsequently declares that it can provide answers to life's questions, even the deepest questions of life. However, the thought that science can save the world is hopelessly optimistic.

Critical

In this era people begin to analyse things more and more and to question authority and traditional belief systems.

However, this era did not produce the harmony that the modern prophets predicted. After two world wars, slavery, communism, Nazism and two nuclear bombs, people began to question whether reason, technology and science could make a better world. In the 21st century the influence of modernism has not ended, though we are in its last days. As modernism falls, so post-modernism rises to take its place.

Representative building

A building that would characterise this period would be the Eiffel Tower. It was built in 1889 and until 1930 was the world's tallest building. It was celebrated as one of modern man's great achievements.

Principle Three: **Post-modern thought**

"Post-modernism" started in the 1960s. Philosophers are not agreed on what to call the period we now live in. Some have suggested the "post post-modern" period. However, when people look back they may well entitle this period "The Disillusionment". Never have so many people been so unhappy and desired something better. In post-modern culture it is easier to proclaim the gospel. With the decline of reason our Christian view is just as relevant as any other religious viewpoint. However, how we initially present it is of great importance. If we strongly assert "the truth" too soon, we are seen as narrow-minded. Post-modern thinking says there is no one truth. An interesting point to note is that other major religions make similar claims.

Post-modern viewpoints

Episodes
In a post-modern world, the meta-narrative is replaced with episodes. This can be seen predominantly through the media. Once, programmes followed a single theme throughout the broadcast; now each programme is broken down into smaller, more manageable portions. We have become a sound-bite generation.

Chance and mystery
Cause and effect have been replaced to a large extent by chance. People have a more fatalistic approach to life. There has been a huge increase in the rise of mysticism (e.g. belief in horoscopes, spiritualism, etc.).

Choice and pleasure
In a post-modern society there is a "pick and mix" approach to life. Post-modern thought states that to choose is to live, and that having no choice is fatal. We are encouraged to live for today and have fun.

However, in post-modernism there are no absolutes. If you want to know what is true then you consult your feelings and make your personal choice.

Representative building
A building that embodies this period is the Millennium Dome. It was built in 1999 and encompassed many different and sometimes contradictory messages. Within a year of its closure it lay empty, unused and semi-derelict!

ASK YOURSELF

Where do you think society is heading? What are some of the dominant values that drive our society today? What are people living for?

Principle Four: Western worldview

Below are some answers to the above questions. Note that not all of Western society's values are negative ones.

Western viewpoints

Reason/rationality
Men and women are able to find the facts/answers to everything.

Experiences
In Western thinking, experiences are vitally important. Whether good or bad, they shape each one of us.

Traditions and superstitions
Halloween, Christmas and Mother's Day play a central part in our culture.

Environment
We are constantly barraged with the problems and potential problems of the environment.

Sex
This is a boom industry in Western culture and invades our lives through the influence of the media.

Money
This drives Western economies. If the stock markets were to collapse what would happen?

Leisure
This is another massive industry. People want more leisure time because they work longer hours. People live for the weekends and their next holiday.

Family upbringing
This affects the way we think and live. We are becoming increasingly individualistic. Yet secretly people long to belong to something.

Spirituality
New Age, Islam and horoscopes play a huge part in Western culture. People are looking for answers in some sort of spirituality. This leads to a problem with the uniqueness of Jesus and Christianity. A belief in one exclusive way to God is not a popular cultural message.

> **ASK YOURSELF**
>
> Are you affected by any of the above values?
>
> Remember, many people under 25 will have post-modern views; those aged 25–50 will have a mixture of post-modern and modern views; and those aged 50 and above may have been taught in schools that focused on modern views.

Principle Five: Christian worldview

Compare Western and Christian worldviews. Paul says in Romans 12:2, "Do not conform any longer to the pattern of this world, but be transformed by the renewing of your mind."

Christian viewpoints

Jesus-centred
All answers are found in Jesus. He is the Son of God.

The Holy Bible
The Bible is absolute truth and therefore is relevant to every generation.

The Church
The Church represents Christ to the world. The local church is the hope for the world.

Faith
This is the opposite of cynicism. How many of us are cynical about our faith?

Vision
God has a plan and a purpose for each one of us.

Humility
This is the opposite of pride.

Service
This is the opposite of status. Loyalty and servanthood are not high values in Western thinking.

Compassion
This is the opposite of selfishness.

Purity/holiness
Living to please God is a completely different outlook on life from that expressed by today's society.

Generosity
This is the opposite of selfishness.

Principle Six: Imposition?

ASK YOURSELF

As you connect with your culture and build relationships with those in your sphere of influence, can you impose your viewpoint on others?

In a post-modern world how can you present the gospel, demonstrate your faith and give people an opportunity to know more about Jesus?

Space for your additional notes

Blowing your cover

Session 4

The Impact of Your Life

Pre-Session Notes

- The approximate time required for this session is one hour, though allow people extra time to complete their testimony.
- Make sure you are familiar with the accompanying Media Pack by watching all the session 4 media clips.
- You will need an actual tract to show the group. There is one available for you to use on the Leader's DVD. Better still, you could produce your own personal tract beforehand.
- The process of producing personal tracts breaks down into the following stages: planning, writing, appraisal of the draft copy, typing on a word processor and printing.
- Some of the group will need help when it comes to the writing stage. Use people in the group who have a flair for writing to help those who struggle in this area.
- At the end of the session encourage everyone to continue to work on their tract.

Welcome

START MEDIA PACK DVD SESSION FOUR – WELCOME

READ OUT

AIMS

1. To understand how your life influences others
2. To write down your personal story
3. To start work on your personal tract

INSTRUCTIONS

- Have the members of the group quote the Bible verse from the previous session to each other and write it in the space provided in their Workbooks. Then reveal the answer using the slide.
- Ask if anybody would like to talk about how God has used them since the last session.

> **Key Scripture**
>
> **Romans 5:8**
>
> 'But God demonstrates his own love for us in this: while we were still sinners, Christ died for us.'
>
> New International Version
>
> Blowing your cover

- Encourage people to be open and honest.

Lifestyle evangelism

INSTRUCTIONS

- Give a few moments for people to write down their answers to the question below.

READ OUT

In the space provided, please write as many common ways of presenting the gospel as you can think of, e.g. in the open air.

- When they have completed this, ask the whole group to come up with a list of all the main ways of presenting the gospel. Then ask people to raise their hand to show by which way they became a Christian.

SO WHAT?

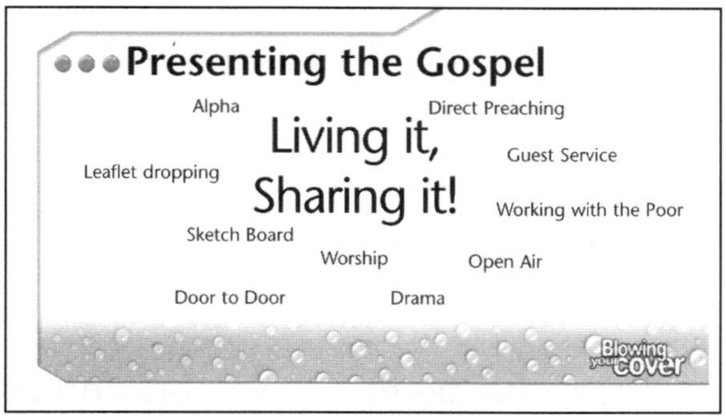

Generally, most people become Christians through friendship evangelism. Ask how many people in the room became Christians because of a friend. Use the slide to emphasise this point.

READ OUT

When we consider the most common ways of presenting the gospel we need to ask the question, "How effective are these methods?"

In a poll of 10,000 people who were asked the question, "What made you first come to church?" the following results were obtained.

INSTRUCTIONS

- The next section reinforces the point further that most people become Christians through friendship. Other forms of evangelism work but we are convinced that most of our evangelism effort should be focused on building relationships.

READ OUT

The table above clearly illustrates how important it is for you to develop friendships with those who don't know Jesus. One way that your life can make an impact on these people is through the power of your own story – both in spoken and written form.

Survey Results

1%	Were contacted through specific outreach
3%	Just walked in
7%	Came because of a special need
8%	Were attracted by the presence of the church and the pastor's ministry
81%	Were invited by relatives and friends

Learning how to write your story

INSTRUCTIONS

- From this point on we concentrate on how to use our conversion story when talking to our non-Christian friends and on how to turn this story into a personal tract.
- Highlight the fact that we have lots of other stories of what God has done in our lives and we should be willing to share these as well.

READ OUT

Spoken and written stories have always played an important part in church history. The apostle Paul on several occasions told his personal story of how Jesus had met with him. The very word "witness" means someone who speaks about things that they have seen, heard and experienced.

SO WHAT?

Friendship evangelism is not just about reaching the three people on everyone's Friendship List. Opportunities to befriend and give away personal tracts come along frequently.

INSTRUCTIONS

- Give the group five minutes to read the Bible verses below and fill in their answers in the Workbook.

READ OUT

Paul developed the practice of telling the story of how he became a Christian and he used it to great effect. Read **Acts 26:12–29** and make a note of the main points of his story.

INSTRUCTIONS

- Discuss how Paul shared his story.
- Emphasise how he broke his story down into manageable portions.
- The next section helps people to write down the main points of their conversion stories.

Writing your story

READ OUT

- It is one of the most powerful and important weapons you have.
- It's a truthful account of how you became a Christian and therefore it is difficult to argue against.
- Let's think – process or event?

SO WHAT?

People become Christians in a variety of ways. For the majority this is usually a process, as people need time to think through the implications of the gospel message. Some become Christians during childhood and for others it is an instant decision. All ways are valid. Ask for a show of hands for process, instant and childhood conversions.

INSTRUCTIONS

- The following section provides helpful questions for people to think through as they prepare their story.

READ OUT

When thinking about your testimony consider the following questions:

Before Conversion (B.C.)

- What was your purpose in life?
- How did you deal with feelings of guilt?
- What was your attitude towards God?
- How did you expect to get to heaven?
- What did you believe about Jesus Christ?
- By what influences and/or experiences did God bring you to faith in Jesus?

During Conversion (D.C.)

- What convinced you that Jesus is God's Son?
- How did he convict you of your sinfulness?
- What led you to rely on Jesus rather than on yourself for a right relationship with God?

- When did you pray to receive Jesus as Saviour and Lord?
- What did you say to God?

After Conversion (A.C.)

- Who is Jesus and how is he your Saviour?
- What does it mean to have him as Lord of your life?
- How is life different since you received Christ?
- What changes have there been in how you live and what you live for?
- What is your relationship with God like?

Important: Do not focus on the sin; instead focus on Christ.

INSTRUCTIONS

- Ask the group to write down their testimonies using the above guidelines. If they became a Christian in their childhood then have them focus on questions 4 and 5 in the Workbooks.
- Walk among the group as they set about this exercise. Watch out for and help those who do not know what to do.

Your Story

- Before you became a Christian (Before Conversion – B.C.)
- Decision Time (During Conversion – D.C.)
- After you became a Christian (After Conversion – A.C.)

Blowing your cover

Practise telling your story

INSTRUCTIONS

- Next, ask for a volunteer to tell their story to everyone. Allow three to four minutes for this and offer lots of encouragement.

MEDIA PACK DVD MOOD ENHANCER 1 – LET'S WRITE YOUR STORY

- Playing length: 25 minutes approimately.

INSTRUCTIONS

- In the Workbook there is an example of a personal tract. Ask everyone to read it. Give them two minutes to do this.

- Then ask the group to comment on its style, content and brevity, etc.

SO WHAT?

When choosing main titles for your tract do not use religious ones. Religious titles put people off. Ask for any questions at this point.

READ OUT

Now it's your turn

Now it is time for you to turn your story into a personal tract. Don't be afraid to have a go. You may be pleasantly surprised at the results. Remember, your story has the potential to impact many people's lives.

Using personal tracts

Once you have written and produced your tract, the vital part comes next – using it! Carry copies with you in a back pocket, diary, handbag or the like. Every day, make sure you take some with you.

Give them to anyone you can (e.g. workmates, fellow students, parents you talk to at the school gate, people at the garage, supermarket, on the train/bus, as well as those on your Friendship List).

INSTRUCTIONS

- Give people at least ten minutes to start to write their tracts. Encourage them to keep working on it and ask if anyone needs help.

Key Scripture

- **Romans 10:9.**

MEDIA PACK DVD SESSION FOUR – CLOSURE

Blowing your cover

Session 5

A Spirit-filled Lifestyle

Pre-Session Notes

- The time needed for this session is one and a half hours.
- Make sure you are familiar with the accompanying Media Pack by watching all the session 5 media clips.
- Everyone will need a Bible for this session, as there are numerous verses to look up.
- Make sure you give adequate time at the end of the session to pray for and minister to one another.

Welcome

START MEDIA PACK DVD SESSION FIVE – WELCOME

READ OUT

AIMS

1. To understand the role the Holy Spirit plays in evangelism
2. To look at the signs that follow your life
3. To pray for your friends

INSTRUCTIONS

- Have the members of the group quote the Bible verse from the previous session to each other and write it in the space provided in their Workbooks. Then reveal the answer using the slide.

Key Scripture

Romans 10:9

'That if you confess with your mouth, "Jesus is Lord," and believe in your heart that God raised him from the dead, you will be saved.'

New International Version

- Ask if anybody would like to talk about how God has used them since the last session.
- Encourage people to be open and honest.

The Holy Spirit

The Holy Spirit

Acts 1:8

'But you will receive power when the Holy Spirit comes on you; and you will be my witnesses in Jerusalem, and in all Judea and Samaria, and to the ends of the earth.'

New International Version

SO WHAT?

Many people may not be fully aware of the vital role that the Holy Spirit plays in evangelism; therefore, we need to examine what the Bible has to say.

INSTRUCTIONS

- Move onto the next slide and ask people to describe some characteristics of the Holy Spirit. Use the slide to enhance the points made.

- Now ask how the Holy Spirit is relevant to evangelism?

- Explain that it is out of our innermost being that "streams of living water flow", as described in **John 7**. Examine the comments made by Jesus in John 7:37–39. If we are not full of God and His Holy Spirit then it becomes very difficult to live a lifestyle of evangelism.

READ OUT

In evangelism the Holy Spirit works in two types of people:

- The unsaved
- The saved

SO WHAT?

God is already working in our lives and in the lives of our unsaved friends. This may be a new concept to some people, therefore help them to grasp it.

READ OUT

Revelation 7:10
"Salvation belongs to our God... "

The whole of the conversion process is full of the activity of the Holy Spirit. He not only works in the messenger as he fills the believer with power, but also is powerfully at work in the life of the hearer (your friends) to whom he brings conviction of sin and, to others, conversion. Truly, salvation belongs to the Lord!

INSTRUCTIONS

- Before moving onto the next paragraph, ask the question, "If salvation belongs to our God", then what part do we play?
- Allow time for discussion and welcome creative ideas and comments.

The Holy Spirit and your friends

READ OUT

As you pray and interact with those on your Friendship List and others that God brings across your path, the Holy Spirit works in two main ways.

INSTRUCTIONS

- Before clicking on to the next slide, ask the group, "What are the two ways that the Holy Spirit works in the lives of those who do not know Jesus?"
- Allow time for a short discussion then click onto the slide below.

READ OUT

SO WHAT?

Knowing that the Holy Spirit convicts and converts takes the weight of the results of evangelism off our shoulders. We are called to be the messenger. This is explained further in the following points.

READ OUT

Firstly, he starts to convict people of their sin. The Holy Spirit not only makes people aware of what is right and wrong but also makes people aware of a coming day of judgement, a time when lives will be evaluated and judged by the living God.

John 16:8

"When he comes, he will convict the world of guilt in regard to sin and righteousness and judgement."

Secondly, the Holy Spirit continues to be actively involved in the lives of some of our non-Christian friends. Out of God's great mercy, the Holy Spirit continues to make people aware of their need for forgiveness and reconciliation. What's more, the Holy Spirit reveals to people that this was all made possible when Christ died on the cross in their place. This continued work of the Holy Spirit eventually leads to their conversion.

INSTRUCTIONS

- Now instruct the group to answer the two questions in their Workbook on how the Holy Spirit convicts and converts people.
- Discuss any issues that this raises.

SO WHAT?

This will help the group to focus on these two important topics.

The Holy Spirit and you

READ OUT

The Holy Spirit not only works in the lives of our unsaved friends, but he also wants to work powerfully in your life as well. Lifestyle evangelism involves displaying the "fruit of the Spirit" as well as the "gifts of the Spirit".

INSTRUCTIONS

- Before looking at how the Holy Spirit fills us with God's power ask the group, "How does the Holy Spirit produce godly character in our lives?" and "What is the result of this fruit?"
- Some helpful answers are that he:
  - Guides us – **John 16:13**
  - Indwells us – **Romans 8:11**
  - Teaches us – **John 14:26**
  - Produces the fruit of the Spirit in us – **Galatians 5:22–23**

MEDIA PACK DVD MOOD ENHANCER 1 – LIVING LETTERS

READ OUT

1 Thessalonians 1:4–5

"For we know, brothers loved by God, that he has chosen you, because our gospel came to you not simply with words, but also with power, with the Holy Spirit and with deep conviction."

Notice that this is also the way Jesus wants us to evangelise. Jesus gave his disciples what they most needed, namely his power and authority. God the Father gave his Son Jesus this power and authority and then Jesus gave this same power and authority to his disciples. So, what is power and authority?

- Power (Greek: *dunamis*) = the ability to do
- Authority (Greek: *exousia*) = the right to do

Jesus gives his disciples (you and me) the power of the Holy Spirit to get the job done as well as His authority to exercise this power.

Having given his disciples power and authority, Jesus then gives his followers specific instructions in how they are to evangelise.

READ OUT

Matthew 10:7

"As you go, preach this message: 'The kingdom of heaven is near.' Heal the sick… "

Notice the phrase, "As you go". These are the same words used in **Matthew 28:18–20** as we read earlier in Session One.

Jesus spent a large proportion of his time bringing truth to people and healing the sick. How do you feel about engaging in such activities?

INSTRUCTIONS

- Encourage the group to be honest and open about this question. Remind them that there will be a time for prayer near the end of the session.

SO WHAT?

As Christians we need to be willing and confident to pray with people about their issues, knowing that God is concerned as much about them as he is about us.

READ OUT

Acts 1:8

"But you will receive power when the Holy Spirit comes on you; and you will be my witnesses in Jerusalem, and in all Judea and Samaria, and to the ends of the earth."

This brings a personal challenge: How full of the Holy Spirit are you?

This statement has been described as the key to the book of Acts. After the day of Pentecost, a timid bunch of deserters were transformed into a dynamic company who marched all around the Mediterranean planting churches in one city after another.

What transformed them?

Where did they get such boldness to speak out about Christ?

Answer: They were **full** of the Holy Spirit.

If we want to fulfil God's plan for our lives and demonstrate the same boldness in our witness to others, then we must experience the Holy Spirit working through our lives, just as the disciples did.

INSTRUCTIONS

- Ask the group to make a note of the different phrases used to describe this experience from the Bible verses found in this section of the Workbook. These verses talk about God's Spirit dwelling within us, helping us to grow and giving them power to share the gospel.

Verses to look up

- Acts 1:5 & Acts 1:8
- Acts 2:4
- Acts 2:17–21
- Acts 2:38
- Acts 10:44–45 & Acts 11:15

READ OUT

The Bible is very clear. In order to live a Spirit-filled lifestyle you need the Holy Spirit working in your life every day.

SO WHAT?

Be confident that the Holy Spirit is already speaking to many of the people in the group. As you move into a prayer/ministry time, ask God to work powerfully. Be expectant.

Let your glory fall

INSTRUCTIONS

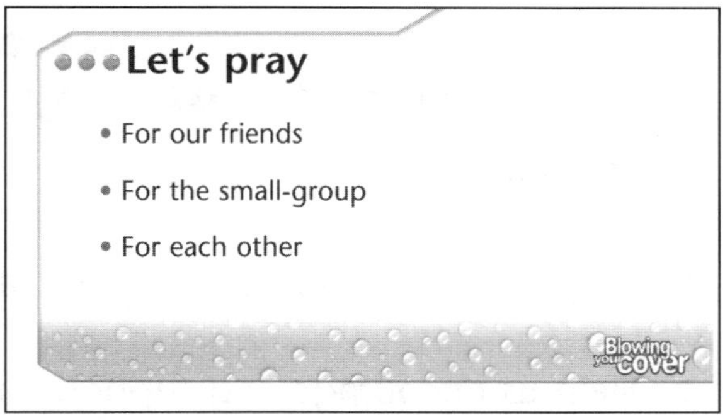

- Now pray together for two things: firstly, for our friends and, secondly, for the other members of your small-group.
- Use the bullet points below to help focus the group's prayers. We suggest you read out the bullets for "our friends" and then pray together.
- Then read out the bullets for the small-group and pray together.

READ OUT

Action point – Let us pray for our friends

Pray for the three people on your Friendship List:

- That God will reveal himself more and that they will be open to his prompting
- That they will see how much better life can be with Christ than without him
- That they will see their need for his forgiveness
- That they will start to understand what Christ did on the cross and its relevance to them
- That they will attend a future Alpha or a similar enquirers' course

READ OUT

Action point – Now let us pray for your small group

Ask God to:

- Help us work together towards leading people to Jesus
- Help us encourage and support each other as we reach out to our friends
- Give wisdom to the group leaders as they seek to guide and advise us
- Give us many encouraging stories in the coming days ahead

INSTRUCTIONS

- Now instruct the group to pair up and pray for each other. Again use the bullet points below to help focus the prayers.
- At this point be available, along with other leaders, to take the initiative in praying for people as God leads you.

READ OUT

Action point –
Now let us pray for each other

Ask God to:

- Give you an anointing for the task
- Help you display the fruit of the Spirit as well as the gifts of the Spirit
- Use you to lead one person to Christ
- Make you open and honest in front of your friends
- Help you live a life consistent with the gospel

Key Scripture

- **Romans 10:13.**

MEDIA PACK DVD SESSION FIVE – CLOSURE

Blowing your cover

Session 6

Blowing Your Cover

Pre-Session Notes

- The time required for this session is one and a half hours.
- Make sure you are familiar with the accompanying Media Pack by watching all the session 6 media clips.
- This session requires a lot of discussion, planning, follow-up and monitoring of the regular socials.
- Small-group leaders need to be reminded that they will be responsible for monitoring the progress of each member of their group.
- At the end of the session find out how people are progressing with their personal tracts.
- There are also course feedback forms on the DVD to allow you to receive feedback from those you have taken through the course. Always be prepared to receive this feedback in order to improve the next time you teach the course.

Welcome

START MEDIA PACK DVD SESSION SIX – WELCOME

READ OUT

AIMS

1. To begin to put into practice what you have learnt so far
2. To enjoy spending time with your friends
3. To overcome fear
4. To blow your cover

INSTRUCTIONS

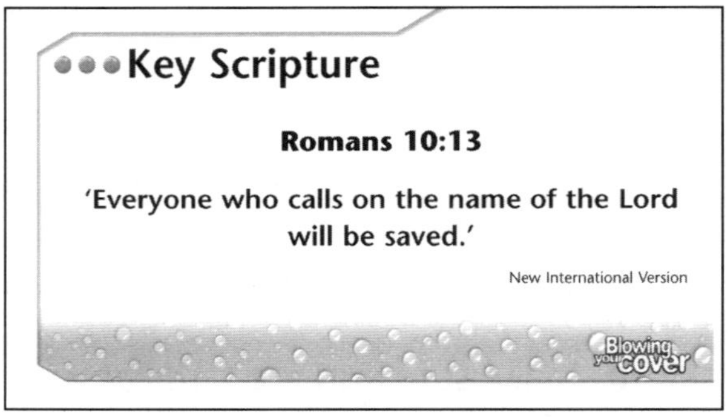

- Have the members of the group quote the Bible verse from the previous session to each other and write it in the space provided in their Workbooks. Then reveal the answer using the slide.
- Ask if anybody would like to talk about how God has used them since the last session.
- Encourage people to be open and honest.

Enjoying your lifestyle of evangelism

READ OUT

This session is all about spending time with your friends on your Friendship List. The focus is not only on inviting these people along to relevant church meetings, but about going out and spending time with them. Remember that throughout the course we have been provoked by the biblical emphasis of "as you go".

> **Enjoying Life**
>
> **John 10:10**
>
> 'The thief comes only to steal and kill and destroy; I have come that they *(God's children)* may have life and have it to the full.'
>
> New International Version
>
> Blowing your cover

The challenge is to introduce other members of your church to your non-Christian friends. This is a BIG mindset change. Let me say it again. The challenge is to introduce other members of your church to your non-Christian friends… not the other way round. Obviously, think carefully about who you will introduce them to.

Your choice may be based on similar interests, or complementary evangelism styles, but whoever you choose they need to be someone you know your non-Christian friends will enjoy meeting.

SO WHAT?

Many Christians are too busy with church activities and need to make lifestyle evangelism one of their priorities in life. Some may need to cut down on the number of Christian meetings they attend in order to have free time to spend with their friends.

Emphasise that we need a "go out from the church" approach (the gospel says "Go"), rather than wait for people to come to us.

READ OUT

Here is a list of suggestions that you could choose from (feel free to be inventive):

- Having a coffee with your friend/s
- Going tenpin bowling
- Doing some aspect of DIY together
- Going shopping with a friend
- Taking your friend and someone else from your group to the local pub's quiz night, or going out for the evening together
- Going to the local park with your friend, your child and their child
- Attending a concert or a sporting event together
- Going to the cinema
- Inviting a friend or neighbour to your house for a meal
- Doing a regular sporting or games activity
- Going for a walk in the countryside
- Taking part in a special interest activity (e.g. surfing, riding and photography)

INSTRUCTIONS

- Now ask everyone to write two activities that they and their friends would enjoy doing.

READ OUT

Remember

You may already be doing some of the things suggested here and developing friendships is a two-way street; be prepared for your friends to invite you out as well.

SO WHAT?

We need to be people who enjoy life. Jesus said he had come that we may have life and life to the full. Enjoying everyday activities should be a large part of a Christian's life. We need to develop larger social lives and possibly reduce the number of church meetings we attend.

Conquering fear

INSTRUCTIONS

- The following section looks at certain obstacles that prevent us from telling others about Jesus. Encourage people to start thinking of issues that prevent them from sharing their faith.

READ OUT

Luke 8:16

"No one lights a lamp and hides it in a jar or puts it under a bed. Instead, he puts it on a stand, so that those who come in can see the light."

The whole aim of Blowing Your Cover is to equip and release you to share your faith confidently and effectively. Having given consideration to what sort of activities you and your friends enjoy, we now want to focus on certain factors that can prevent us from meeting together. Some of these issues are simple practical matters; for instance, organising the time and place to meet one of the people on your Friendship List for a cup of coffee. Hopefully, these issues are easily dealt with; however, there are harder issues for some people.

SO WHAT?

Fear can paralyse your faith. Remember, the people on our Friendship Lists want to spend time with us because they are our friends. They won't if we treat them as projects.

INSTRUCTIONS

- Use this slide to show that there are many different excuses we can make.

READ OUT

What sort of things would stop you from inviting a friend to attend the next Alpha or similar enquirers' course?

In the boxes below write down as many excuses as you can think of:

Excuses, excuses and excuses... **Big excuse: FEAR**.

INSTRUCTIONS

- At this point ask the group to list reasons that prevent them from sharing their faith with a friend or even inviting relevant friends to an Alpha course or similar enquirers' course. Some of the fears could be fear of losing that friendship, or fear of being perceived as strange. Give time for them to write down their answers.

- Discuss together why fear is such a big issue.

READ OUT

What is fear?

- **F**alse
- **E**xpectations
- **A**ppearing
- **R**eal

Someone once said that fear can come from our false expectations appearing real to each one of us. For instance, sometimes we don't bother asking people to meet us because our expectation is low. We automatically assume that people will say no when we ask them and often we don't bother to offer an invitation. This is wrong thinking. Because we are fishing in our "sphere of influence" (people we already have relationships with), just about everyone we ask may well respond positively to invitations. Be aware of wrong expectations.

"Let me assert my firm belief that the only thing we have to fear is fear itself."
Franklin D. Roosevelt (1882–1945), US Democratic president.
First Inaugural Address, 4 March 1933

Fear can make us feel inadequate. We can be paralysed by thoughts such as, "What would I say to someone?" or "I don't think I am particularly good at communicating well with others; I get completely tongue-tied." Others think, "What if they reject me or don't want to listen to what I want to say? I would feel such a failure."

SO WHAT?

FEAR OF BEING INADEQUATE

Opportunities to speak and communicate relevant truths can be missed because we think we are theological lightweights! Rather than being concerned about what we do not know, we can communicate what we do know. Remember, Jesus taught profound truths in simple ways. So, start with your own story and if specific questions arise feel quite free to say, "Sorry, I don't know the answer." But at the same time be determined to do some homework and find the answer before you meet up again.

FEAR OF LOSING OUR REPUTATION

We are often concerned about what others will think of us. Jesus' example in **Philippians 2:7** is very provoking: "… he made himself nothing." All too often we can be paralysed by such thoughts as, "What would I say to someone?" or miss an opportunity because we feel, "I get completely tongue-tied." If we are serious about being effective, we must be prepared to look foolish.

READ OUT

Be encouraged. Jeremiah had to deal with the same issues:

Jeremiah 1:6

"Ah, Sovereign LORD," I said, "I do not know how to speak;
I am only a child."

How did God respond to Jeremiah? See **Jeremiah 1:7–10**.

INSTRUCTIONS

- Instruct the group to write the answer to the above question in the space provided in their Workbook.

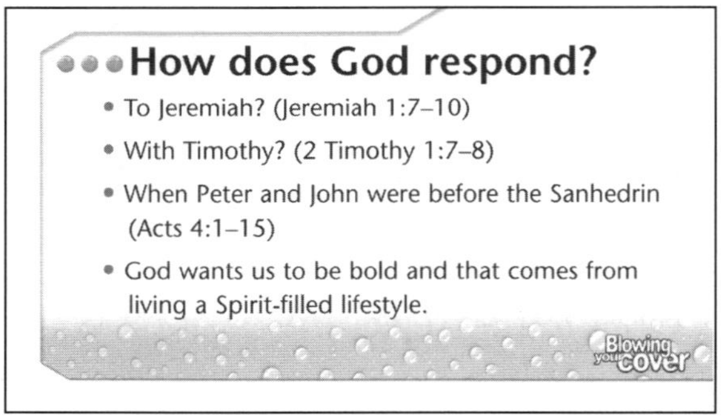

READ OUT

The most important thing to remember as you engage in doing things that do not come easily is to know that God is with you. He is the one who helps you overcome timidity and fear. Your only requirement is to trust God. As you yield to God's control, he provides the opportunity, the power and the words. And even if one or two of your friends say, "Sorry, I can't come this time," you have nothing to feel bad about. It is normal! No one can realistically attend everything. Taking this approach helps you to avoid disappointment.

2 Timothy 1:7–8

"For God did not give us a spirit of timidity, but a spirit of power, of love and of self-discipline. So do not be ashamed to testify about our Lord… "

INSTRUCTIONS

- Now ask the group to read **Acts 4:1–15** and then write down what they learn about the boldness of Peter and John before the Sanhedrin in the space provided in their Workbooks.

READ OUT

God wants you to be bold. He also wants you to believe that several of your friends will gladly enjoy your company and in time attend an Alpha or similar enquirers' course. Like Peter and John, we need to know that this boldness comes from being filled with the Holy Spirit. You need to be filled daily with the Holy Spirit and be ready to stand up and be counted.

Ezekiel 22:30

"I looked for a man among them who would build up the wall and stand before me in the gap..."

SO WHAT?

- Boldness comes from God. To live a lifestyle of evangelism in front of our friends we need to be men and women who are continually filled with the Holy Spirit (**Ephesians 5:18**) and willing to stand in that gap.

MEDIA PACK DVD MOOD ENHANCER 1 – MULTI-STOREY

Your checklist

READ OUT

You will be encouraged to meet up with your friends on a regular basis, and to spend quality time praying for them. Remember, these times should not add additional pressure to your life, but be something that you do naturally. In your group meetings you should pray for all the combined names on the group's Friendship List.

Finally, to help you monitor your progress and to apply everything you have learnt a checklist is included.

It will expose areas in your life where you need help in evangelism. Remember, other members of the group have complementary styles that will help you in your witness to others. You are not meant to fish for people on your own. We are encouraged to fish together. We need each other. Biblical "fishing for men" is a community activity, not "one man and his rod!" Jesus always sent people out in pairs. He sent his disciples out in pairs for all sorts of tasks – to participate in village evangelism, to secure the use of a room for the Passover meal and even to collect a donkey for him to ride on into Jerusalem!

Biblical evangelism means working mainly as a team, not on your own.

INSTRUCTIONS

- Now introduce the checklist to the group and click onto the next slide.

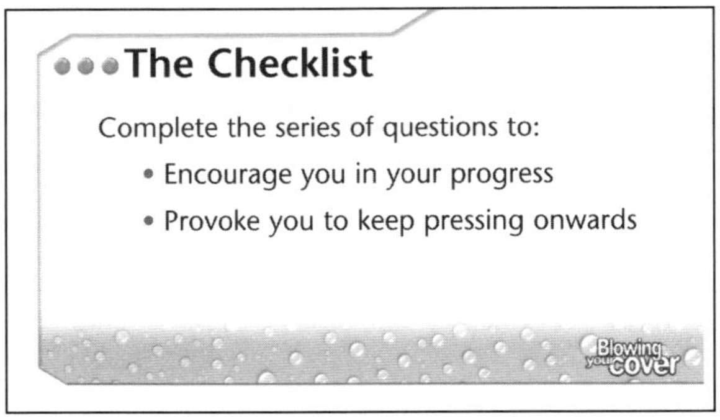

The checklist

The following checklist will help you monitor your progress. When reviewing these questions tick the line for encouragement and let the unticked lines bring the challenge.

____ Do you know the main evangelism "style" of at least three other friends in your church?

____ Are you aware of two others whose "style" complements your "style" of evangelism?

____ Are you praying regularly for the three people on your Friendship List?

____ Have you recently enjoyed spending time with any of the three names on your Friendship List – for instance, lunch, coffee or a chance meeting?

____ Are you learning to listen actively to your friends?

____ Have you had a good conversation with any of these three people recently?

____ Did you turn any of these conversations towards biblical truths?

____ Have you had an opportunity in the last month to pass on your story to any of your non-Christian friends?

____ Have you introduced any of your church friends to the people on your Friendship List?

____ Have you finished writing up your personal tract?

____ Have you had your personal tract printed (e.g. using a computer)?

____ Have you given a copy of your personal tract to a non-Christian since you last reviewed this checklist?

____ Have you shared the "picture gospel outline" with anyone on your Friendship List?

____ Have you prayed WITH any of your friends recently?

____ Have you ever invited any of the above to an Alpha or similar enquirers course?

____ Have you been that all-important "link in the chain"?

____ Have you seen anyone on your Friendship List become a Christian?

INSTRUCTIONS

- Now ask everyone to complete the checklist in their Workbooks. Let the ticked boxes bring encouragement and the unticked ones bring the challenge.

- It is vital that you, the trainer, complete this checklist too. Lead by example.

We recommend the following:

- Once a month an evening should be given over to reviewing how all the group members are progressing with the people on their Friendship Lists. This will involve talking, feedback, praying for these people and finding out who has introduced anyone else in the group to their friends.

- Members need to regularly review their checklists.

- Expect encouraging stories to filter through the church.

- For everyone to spend the necessary time in prayer and contact with unbelievers.

What happens next?

MEDIA PACK DVD SESSION SIX – CLOSURE

PART THREE
Producing Personal Tracts

Welcome

This part of the Leader's Guide deals with the presentation and production of a personal tract. It relates to Session Four of the course Workbook. Remember, all the concepts relating to writing personal tracts are covered on the Blowing Your Cover Leader's DVD. This section provides guidelines, tips and hints on how to transform a written testimony into an attention-grabbing personal tract that you would feel comfortable handing out to your family, friends and the other people you meet.

After completing the Blowing Your Cover course, most participants should have composed the contents of their personal tract. At this point you have to think about the production and presentation aspects. There is nothing worse than being handed a piece of paper with either too much writing on, or one where the writing is too small or difficult to read. Remember, the quality and appearance of personal tracts matters. What's more, the size of your personal tract is important too! It needs to fit easily into a pocket or small bag without being badly damaged.

The physical size

One suggested format that could be used for producing personal tracts is 12.6 cm long x 8.8 cm high (this is a frequently used size). It has a vertical fold (lengthways) across the middle. Feel free to use whatever dimensions and format you wish but remember there are principles to work to, as mentioned above. Be creative and do not be afraid to experiment if you have the time and inclination.

Four panels

Once the paper or card has been folded in half you have four panels (two on each side of the paper or card, as illustrated). The first panel acts as a cover and the remaining three contain the written text and information details. Let us look at the first panel in detail, as essentially this is the first thing people will see when you hand it over. We want people to turn the page and keep reading.

The first panel

The first panel should ideally have a picture of you, but this is not a hard and fast rule. A portrait shot is usually the best although not essential; if you have one that helps illustrate your story that's even better. For instance, one example of a personal tract is that of a man dressed in a prisoner's outfit and the title underneath the picture is "I've been set free!" Other ideas could be to use a caricature or, if you are adamant that you do not want a picture of yourself in any form on the cover, then

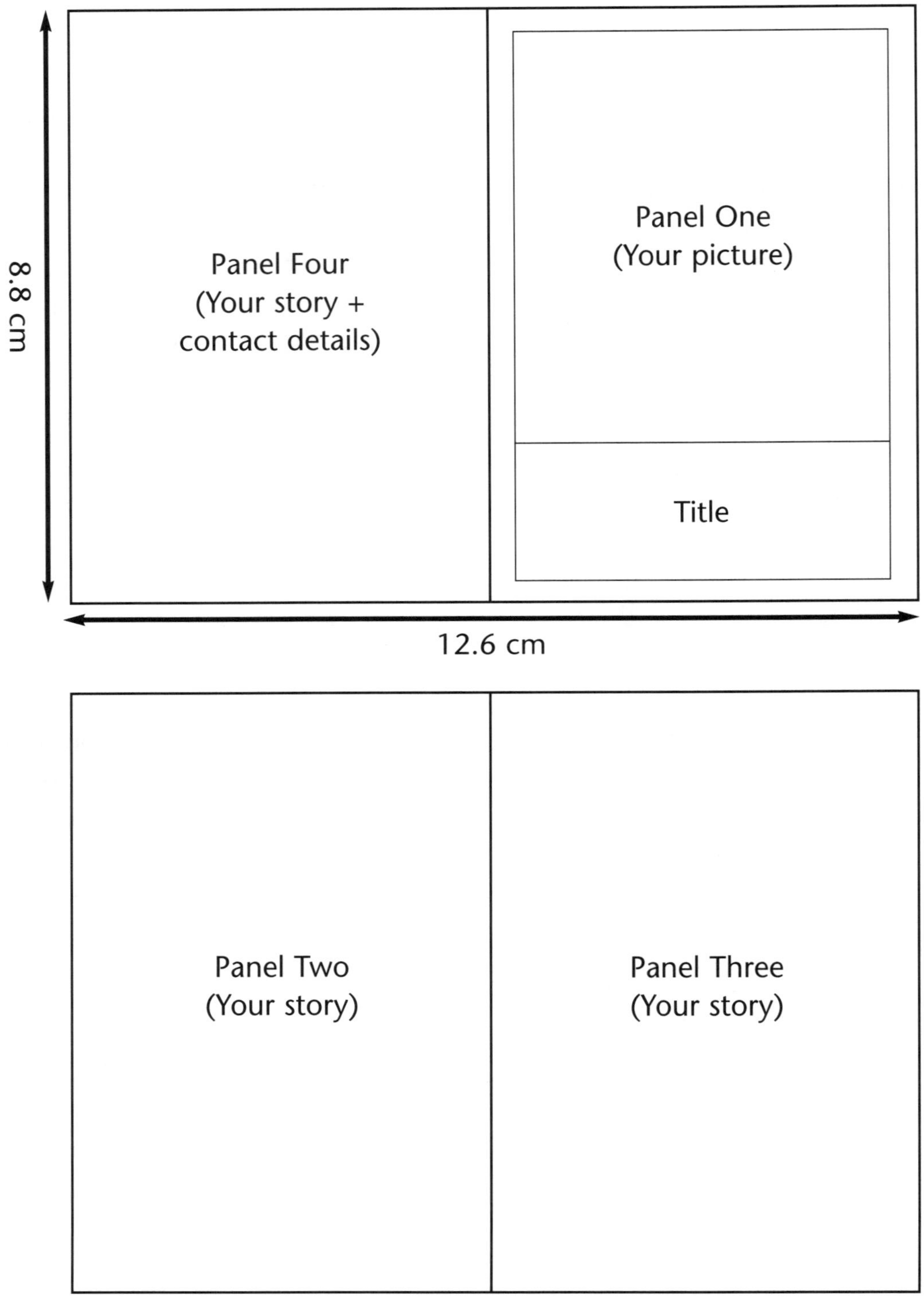

a suitable graphic or piece of clip art can be used. Be creative and innovative. Do not leave it blank. If you can, use colour photos and pictures, as they will catch the eye of the recipient.

For the final touch, a title is necessary, something short and snappy that will grab the reader's attention and encourage them to read more. Make the title relevant to your story. It cannot be stressed how important it is to leave out any religious jargon or corny/cheesy phrases as this could consign all the hard work to the nearest rubbish bin.

Panels two, three and four

This is where your story fits. As you can see, you do not have much space. Use around 450 words; this includes contact details. Please note that space disappears at an alarming rate!

An important aspect is to use a simple and clear font. The font you select needs to be clear and easy to read with no fancy squiggles or complex lettering. The size of the font is extremely important too. Do not make it so small that the reader will need a magnifying glass to read it, or so large that the story loses its punch and important details.

A word about desktop publishing

Today's desktop publishing applications have a number of utilities that can manipulate text. When producing personal tracts adhere to the principle of keeping everything simple and clear, as this will minimise the number of reworks required and personal time reformatting it. Arial font was used in the sample tract.

Keep a margin around the text and preferably around the picture too. Try not to leave any stray, small amounts of text on one page. Use bold, italic, underlining and colour sparingly. One suggested area where colour could be useful is for the contact details. We want to give the reader every opportunity to know where to contact us when they show interest.

On the Blowing Your Cover Leader's DVD there is copy of the sample personal tract in the "Personal Tract" folder along with templates to give you a head start. They are in a Microsoft® Publisher® 2000 format.

Bibliography

We would like to acknowledge and recommend the following resources. They have helped shape our thinking and will provide further stimulus to any reader.

Aldrich, Joseph C.; *Lifestyle Evangelism*, Multnomah Press, 1999
Allan, John; *Just Looking*, Bible Society, 1987
Bell, Arnold; *Postmodernism* Stoneleigh Tape, Newfrontiers,*1997*
Bruce, F.F.; *The Spreading Flame*, Paternoster Press, 1964
Chantry, Walter; *Today's Gospel: Authentic or Synthetic?*, Banner of Truth Trust, 1996
Coleman, Robert; *The Master Plan of Evangelism*, Revell, 1986
Drummond, Lewis A.; *The Evangelist: The Worldwide Impact of Billy Graham*, Word, 2001
Edwins, Dave; *Moorlands College Level 2 Evangelism Notes*, 2002
Ford, Kevin; *Jesus for a New Generation*, IVP, 1995
Frost, Rob; *Pilgrims*, Kingsway
Green, Michael; *Evangelism Now and Then*, IVP, 1979
Green, Michael; *Critical Choices*, Hodder & Stoughton
Gumbel, Nicky; *Telling Others: The Alpha Initiative*, Alpha Products, 1994
Houston, Brian; *For This Cause*, Maximised Leadership Series, 2001
Hull, Bill; *The Disciple-Making Pastor*, Revell, 1999
Mahaney, C.J.; *Why Small Groups?*, PDI, 1996
Manley Pippert, Rebecca; *Out of the Salt Shaker*, IVP, 1999
Mittleberg, Strobel and Hybels; *Becoming a Contagious Christian*, Zondervan, 1996
Nouwen, Henri J.M.; *In The Name of Jesus*, Darton, Longman & Todd, 1989
Peterson, Jim; *Evangelism as a Lifestyle*, Navpress, 1980
Pollard, Nick; *Evangelism Made Slightly Less Difficult*, IVP, 1997
Singlehurst, Laurence; *Sowing Reaping Keeping*, Crossways Books, 1995
Sjogren, Steve, *Irresistable Evangelism*, Group publishing, 2004
Snyder, Howard A *et al.*; *The Radical Wesley and Patterns for Church Renewal*, IVP, 1980
Sprenger, Mike; *Total Evangelism*, Newfrontiers
Strobel, Lee; *Inside the Mind of Unchurched Harry and Mary*, Zondervan, 1993
Tomczak, Larry; *Divine Appointments*, Kingsway, 1986
Virgo, Terry; *Weak People Mighty God*, Kingsway, 1990
Wimber, John; *Power Evangelism*, Hodder & Stoughton, 2001
Wright, N.T.; *Jesus and the Victory of God*, SPCK, 1996
Yancey, Philip; *What's So Amazing about Grace?*, HarperCollins, 1997